NICARAGUA

Julia and Peter Menard-Warwick

PIKA PRESS

ISBN 0-918957-07-9

First printing November, 1989

Printed in the United States of America

Pika Press
203 E. Main — P.O. Box 457
Enterprise, Oregon 97828

ACKNOWLEDGEMENTS

We would like to express our sincere gratitude to the Paz de Cristo group of St. Joseph's Church, Seattle, Washington, and also to Julia's grandmother, Billie Vincent, for helping to distribute these letters during our time in Nicaragua.

*How does one hate a country, or love one?... I lack the trick of it.
I know people, I know towns, farms, hills and rivers and rocks,
I know how the sun at sunset in autumn falls on the side of a
certain plowland in the hills; but what is the sense of giving a
boundary to all that, of giving it a name and ceasing to love where
the name ceases to apply?*

Ursula K. Le Guin
The Left Hand of Darkness

INTRODUCTION

I have a friend named Mary Chatlos, who looks like anybody's mom. She worked for the Internal Revenue Service for thirty years or so before taking early retirement and going to work for the peace movement. In 1984-85, she spent a year in the war zone in Nicaragua, working with the faith-based human rights group, Witness for Peace. After she came back to the States she used to go and speak about her experiences and show her slides to church groups, etc. And she'd do so with her heart on her sleeve, because her year there had meant a lot to her, and she'd seen a lot of people suffering as a result of US policy in Central America. And after her talks, often some nice parishioner would come up to her and say in a puzzled voice "You know, I'm sorry but I just can't tell who to believe!" At which point she would try not to feel insulted as she thought to herself "Well, why don't you believe me?"

Part of the tragedy of Nicaragua in the 1980s, certainly part of the reason that the war has continued so long, is that the voices that have most successfully defined the public view of Nicaragua in the United States have been those of politicians who have never been there, or of reporters who have done a lot of their research from the bar at the Hotel Intercontinental in Managua. Voices like Mary's have not been heard so loudly and have often been dismissed as "biased" or "duped." And yet they have been heard, directly through slide shows, and indirectly through people who went to a slide show and then attended a demonstration or called their congressperson. And if the US has not been successful in reimposing its will on Nicaragua in the years since 1979, this is partly why.

We were in Nicaragua from January to December of 1988. I was teaching English to students training to be professional translators at the Jesuit-run Universidad Centroamericana in Managua, while my husband Peter was helping to build a school for mentally-handicapped teenagers. We had wanted to come back to Nicaragua since a two-week trip we'd made there in November of 1985 following a month of doing human rights work in Guatemala—we'd been struck by the contrast between the two countries. Guatemala has a lovely cool climate ("the eternal springtime"), pine-forested mountains, Indian women in beautiful hand-embroidered clothing. But we'd also met a woman there who'd received death threats from the government security forces for working as a health educator: because she was telling people to dig latrines and boil water, she was considered a political subversive. And the streets of Guatemala City were full of sleek cars and children begging.

After that experience, it was perhaps more striking to us than it would have been otherwise to visit a government-sponsored school-lunch program in Ocotal, Nicaragua, and to realize that the only people on the streets begging were old winos. The Maryknoll nun I met who worked in a clinic in the same town told me that though the government bureaucracy was occasionally a headache, they were very supportive of the work she was doing, both in health education and direct care—public health has always been a priority of the current Nicaraguan government.

At the same time I was struck by the very obvious political polarization of the country. Pro and anti-government graffiti was visible everywhere. When I went into a photocopy shop, I saw derisively anti-government cartoons posted prominently all over the walls—something you did not see in the climate of terror prevailing in Guatemala. Signs of the war were also visible. Anti-government *contra* rebel forces had attacked the town a year and a half earlier, and ruins of the buildings they'd blown up were still standing. We ate dinner one evening at the nightclub where a local *contra* supporter had tossed a hand grenade into the middle of a high school dance, killing six students.

It was these experiences that led me, as I was finishing my

Masters program in 1987, to apply for work in Nicaragua. After I'd received a job offer at the University, Peter met Frances Romero, a woman from the US who'd lived in Nicaragua for five years and was back in Seattle visiting. She was looking for volunteer help with her efforts to provide facilities for mentally-handicapped youth; the school they were building was just outside Managua where the University was located. We had bad memories of the Managua heat and traffic, but figured we could get used to it, and we were sure that whatever else it might be, a year in Nicaragua would be a great learning experience.

These letters, then, are a record of what we learned in a year of living in Nicaragua. We wrote them partly because we were simply homesick and wanting to stay connected to people we'd left in the United States, but also because we figured that it was important to send back first-hand accounts of the situation in Nicaragua to counteract the Reagan administration and even the *New York Times* version of events there. Realizing we were lousy photographers, we knew we'd never put together a great slide show—we'd have to present what we saw in writing.

In many ways our visit in 1985 had prepared us for what we were to find. The Managua heat was oppressive, the government bureaucracy was occasionally a headache, the war in the mountains exercised a profound influence on national life, the government and indeed the citizenry were still interested in public health (Nicaragua is probably the only country in the world where English teachers have their students clamoring to do reports on infant diarrhea). The one major difference we found to our first impressions was that by 1988 the Nicaraguan economy had deteriorated to the point where there were sizable numbers of children begging in the streets.

So that was how we got to Nicaragua. But how did Nicaragua get to the point where we saw it in 1988? Almost all Nicaraguans, and very few North Americans, know the history of US involvement in that country since the 19th century. And it's impossible to understand Nicaragua in 1988 without knowing a little of its history, which of course resembles in many ways the history of the rest of Latin America.

Five hundred years ago, the Indians in Nicaragua were

invaded and colonized by the Spanish conquistadors. The society has been stratified ever since, with a wealthy upper and small middle class of mostly European descent, and a large poor majority descended primarily from the Indians. In 1810, Spain gave up its Latin American holdings, and throughout the 19th and early 20th century, the United States became more and more involved in the area, helping presidents to come to power and then deposing them again when they acted contrary to US interests. The US Marines invaded the country three times in the early 20th century, occupying it throughout most of the 1920s. They were there to contain unrest, but they faced ever-increasing opposition from the Nicaraguan people and especially from the small guerrilla army led by Augusto Cesar Sandino, a small man in a big hat, a nationalist and a theosophist, who operated out of the mountains of the north and jungles of the east, fighting the US Marines to a standstill.

Unable to counter the growing wave of nationalism, the US changed tactics, creating and training the Nicaraguan National Guard, under the leadership of Anastasio Somoza. The US troops pulled out of Nicaragua, and Somoza had Sandino assassinated. About Somoza, Franklin D. Roosevelt once said "He may be a son of a bitch, but he's our son of a bitch"— and Nicaragua has never forgotten that. Somoza set up a dynasty which survived his own assassination and lasted for over forty years under two of his sons.

In 1961, Carlos Fonseca and eleven other students from the University in León founded the Sandinista National Liberation Front (FSLN), in memory of Sandino, to fight for the overthrow of the brutal National Guard and the Somoza dynasty, which by now owned a large share of the Nicaraguan land and economy. The Sandinista movement grew slowly, setting up guerrilla base camps in the mountains and doing underground organizing in the cities. This was risky work—only one of the twelve founders of the FSLN survived to see victory.

Victory might never have come if it hadn't been for the 1972 earthquake that destroyed 80% of Managua, the capital city. Afterwards no one could forget that Somoza and his cronies had pocketed the relief funds that came in from abroad. Downtown Managua is still in ruins today as an ever-present reminder of that. But it was not until the assassination of liberal opposition leader Pedro Joaquín Chamorro in 1978 at the hands of Somoza's agents that the leaders of the middle-class business community decided to join with the Sandinistas in carrying out Somoza's overthrow. And meanwhile neighborhood kids in the poor barrios, inspired by the Sandinistas, were rising against the National Guard with rocks and homemade bombs. In the spring of '79, Jimmy Carter saw the writing on the wall and cut aid to the dictatorship, on July 17 Somoza fled the country, and on July 19 the Sandinistas took Managua. They've been the government ever since, receiving 60% of the vote in the 1984 elections. Fifty thousand had died in the war, many of them teenagers.

As many people are saying now, "that was the easy part."

The hard part is rebuilding the country and trying to create a just and democratic society in a nation that has been so unjust for so long. The Revolution is a powerful ideal in the process of being realized, and of course often betrayed. The guns and bombs and rocks and neighborhood organizing were not the Revolution in themselves, but only created the conditions for this long-haul effort to reshape society. The Revolution is thus known as "the process," and people both Nicaraguan and foreign who are supportive of the Revolution often describe themselves as being "with the process."

So what does this process involve? At its heart is the creation of the New Man and the New Woman who will build and inhabit the new society. This involves inner transformation, as much Christian as Marxist, towards an ideal of self-sacrifice and dedication to the community. More concretely, this ideal involves the promotion of public health, clean water systems, nutritional education, free clinics. It calls for equal access to education, from basic literacy to the university level. Furthermore, this revolutionary ideal seeks to create a New Nicaragua in which women have equal rights, in which no one goes hungry or lives in sub-standard housing, in which land is turned over to the *campesinos* to cultivate. The revolution, moreover, seeks to do this in a context of pluralism and democracy in which different voices are heard and respected, and people are encouraged to think for themselves. Above all, the Nicaraguan revolution is nationalist, attempting to escape from centuries of domination by more powerful nations, to rediscover authentic Nicaraguan culture, and to make decisions that will benefit Nicaraguans and not the stockholders of multinational corporations or the campaign prospects of US political leaders.

This is the ideal that the Sandinistas have struggled to put into practice for ten years. Along the way there's been success, failure, hypocrisy, dedication, laziness, hard work, mistakes made and lives lost. At this point it seems possible that their hopes for a New Nicaragua will never be fulfilled. And yet the ideal of the revolution goes on, and it will continue to live as long as anyone is still working (one step forward, two steps back) to implement it.

The biggest reason that their dream is so far from reality has been US pressure. Jimmy Carter aided the new Sandinista government; one of Ronald Reagan's first acts in office was to put a stop to that. The CIA was meanwhile arming and training the remnants of the National Guard in hopes of overthrowing the Sandinistas militarily. In 1981 the war began all over again, with the US backed *contras* (or "counter-revolutionaries") attacking Nicaragua from their bases in neighboring Honduras. In 1985 the US imposed a trade embargo against Nicaragua and in 1987 the five Central American presidents meeting together signed the Esquipulas Accords, laying the groundwork and raising hopes for a negotiated settlement of the conflict.

Nevertheless, the war had already had a devastating effect on Nicaragua. Thousands of people were dead, many of them civilians in remote rural areas killed by the *contras* for cooperating with Sandinista programs (such as vaccination campaigns). Thousands more had been kidnapped, and their whereabouts are still unknown. Precious resources had been diverted from development to defense, making it impossible to carry out programs to fulfill the hopes raised by the revolution.

Possibly the worst effect of the US pressure, however, has been the kind of long-term damage to the economy that I go on at length about in these letters. Undeniably, some of the blame for the inflation and shortages can go to Sandinista mismanagement, and some of it to droughts in '86 and '87, and floods and hurricane in '88; nevertheless, it is also true that part of the US military strategy has been to hurt the Nicaraguan economy in order to increase discontent with the Sandinistas and to wear people down with the stress of daily living till they no longer have the energy to go on with the Revolution. To some extent this has been successful—a lot of people are very ready to blame the government for the economic mess and to do so loudly and publicly. Many people will say that the Sandinistas are a bunch of crooks, or (as a soft-drink vendor once told us) that President Daniel Ortega is a "retard."

Under the present circumstances, with life in Nicaragua as hard as it is today, the Sandinista ideal of self-sacrifice for the good of the community is a very high ideal indeed and very difficult to live up to—many Nicaraguans admire it, but few try to carry it out. Within the Sandinista movement itself, there are some who are shining examples of hard work and dedication, while there are unfortunately others who can only be described as *oportunistas*. Most Nicaraguans, like most people everywhere, are essentially selfish, just trying to get by and feed their families under very difficult circumstances. And it's hard to blame them. At the same time, however, it's very clear that for the Revolution to work, for Nicaragua to have a better future, it's going to be necessary for people to transcend ordinary human selfishness and unite for the good of the community.

Selfishness in Nicaragua is visible and ugly, and it's very obvious what its effects are on society. Every time I elbowed the person next to me in order to get a better position on the bus or a better tomato at the supermarket, I was very aware that we were competing for scarce resources, and that I didn't want to lose out. The many who profit by the inflationary spiral while others suffer are an example of the same thing. You can see such people on every street corner in Managua, and there were times during the year when I felt that the law of the jungle had entirely overcome all cooperative and revolutionary sentiment. And then I would be confronted with examples of the revolutionary ideal in action—middle-class university students from safe, muggy Managua volunteering to pick coffee in the chilly mountains of Jinotega, where they are subject to *contra* attacks, where their only diet is rice and beans, where there are never enough blankets to go around. It's this spirit that could save Nicaragua in the end.

And the conclusion I came to finally, although it took a hurricane to pound this into my head, is that the selfish people suffer the most. After the hurricane I had my beginning composition students write a paragraph with the topic sentence: "The hurricane was a _____ experience for me." Almost without exception, the ones who had participated in relief brigades wrote "The hurricane was a wonderful experience," while those who had sat at home and worried said that it was a "terrible experience." Often in a short-term crisis, people will stop grasping at their own personal happiness and work together to help those in need.

And often this is remembered as a time of real joy. But in Nicaragua, every day is a crisis, and the people I met who were coping with this best were those who were working, against the odds, to make the Revolution a reality. They were the ones who had a sense of hope even though times were dark. Otherwise life in Nicaragua is reduced to a grim struggle over tomatoes.

Strangely, the thing I miss most about Nicaragua is that sense of hope, that sense of people working together against the odds to make things better, and perhaps above all the sense that ordinary work (e.g. teaching English) done well is a way to build the Revolution, to bring about a brighter future. People in the US too often feel as though they "can't make a difference," whereas in Nicaragua individual effort can be easily seen to be part of a larger effort to construct the future. Despite all of the discouragement and hypocrisy, the Revolution is a living thing.

Once, in observing a colleague's English class, I listened in on a discussion by a group of mostly women students on the difficulty of getting men to help with the housework. And one of them said "Well, it may look impossible now, but you know, back in 1977, no one thought Somoza would ever be overthrown...."

No matter how discouraged Nicaraguans may get with Nicaragua in the 1980s or 90s, they nonetheless have the precious memory of having once done the impossible.

I hope they can do it again. And I hope that these letters,

joining with other voices, can help to create an opening in US foreign policy that will allow them to do so—to build the New Nicaragua for which so many have struggled.

Julia Menard-Warwick
Bellingham, Washington
July 1989

MANAGUA, NICARAGUA
February 7, 1988

Dear Friends and Family,

We've been in Nicaragua two weeks now and are starting to get settled in. This is the first of, I hope, many newsletters that I plan to write in the next year. I also hope to write to most of you individually, and would be truly delighted to get letters from any of you. We would also be overjoyed to see any of you down here for a visit. I miss you all.

Peter and I have both started to work. I'm going to be teaching English to students training to be professional translators at the Jesuit university here in Managua. Although the classes I'm teaching don't start till March 14th, at this point I'm involved with planning meetings and materials development for the up-coming school year. Things are a little slow right now, and I'm looking forward to getting into the classroom. Peter's working with the Seattle Construction Brigade building a school for mentally handicapped teenagers; the brigade goes home in a month, but he will stay on with the project. His work is going a bit slow now, too, due to a lack of construction materials, but he's also started working with some of the kids and will probably be teaching carpentry to the more advanced ones when their educational program gets under-way in March.

Managua is a pretty town, for the most part, with palm trees, flowers, and views of lakes and hills. The weather is warm, humid, and windy, but not too hot yet. We've been getting around by bicycle as the buses are so crowded that they don't even stop most of the time. It's a little scary riding on cob-blestoned streets with no shoulder, as big trucks roar by us blasting diesel fumes, but we're getting used to it. The house we're living in is in a middle-class neighborhood with tree-lined streets not too far from the university; we're renting a room from an elderly widow who needs the income to keep the house in repair. She's a sweet person, and we're quite comfortable here.

People here were very pleased by the recent defeat of *contra* aid, of course, although it's disappointing that the vote was so close. Twice last week on the evening news there were reports of *contra* attacks on agricultural cooperatives; we saw TV footage of little houses riddled with bullets and bodies laid out on the ground. Eleven civilians were killed on Tuesday, including four children, and seventeen were killed on Thursday, including an eight month old baby. As I heard one person say, "If the US Congress was really concerned with morality, they wouldn't even consider giving money to those terrorists." And a number of people have expressed anger that the Congress feels as though it has the right to decide the future of Nicaragua. "This is our country," people say. "We don't tell them how to run their country..."

Most of all though, it seems as if people here are really sick of the war. We went to a demonstration in front of the US Embassy to celebrate the defeat of *contra* aid. There was a choir of teenagers there, singing songs of revolution and songs of peace. Some of them were just about to be drafted into the army. The song that moved me most said "We don't want any more heroes." This is a country that's really proud of its heroes, but all too often here, "hero" means "martyr." At the same time, this exhaustion with the war has led to real optimism about the peace process in Central America. The Sandinistas look upon it as *their* peace process, and call for a negotiated settlement in all of their public pronouncements. At the same time they emphasize, however, that what they want is *una paz digna*—peace with dignity.

Meanwhile, the economy here is in shambles, due to the war, the US trade embargo, the world price of coffee, etc. Unemployment isn't the problem. Instead there's a labor shortage, which means that people get promoted into jobs they're not qualified for. A lot of skilled professional and technical people have moved to Miami in the last few years, and a lot of young people are in the Army. Among other things, there's a shortage of English teachers, which means that I feel very welcome here. At the same time, inflation is running at 1000%. Consumer goods, such as toilet paper, are in short supply, and what's available is very expensive for the average person. The government supplies rations of basic food items at subsidized prices, and that's the only way that most people keep their heads above water. Five hundred thousand *cordobas** is a pretty normal wage right now, and a pound of beans at the unsubsidized, free market price costs 11,000. It's as if someone in the States who earns $1000 a month had to pay twenty dollars a pound for beans. At this point, we're paying the unsubsidized prices and are looking forward to getting our resident ID cards so we can take advantage of the rationing. Although I hear you have to wait in line.

There's also an Energy Crisis on at the moment. Cars can wait in line up to a day and a half to buy gas. A number of major industries are temporarily shut down or running on half capacity because of lack of electricity. At my work and in all government offices, the power goes off at 1 P.M. every day. Where we live, it's usually off in the morning. Water is in short supply as well; it's turned off two days a week depending on the neighborhood, which means filling buckets the night before. The good thing about the water, though, is that it's pure enough to drink right out of the tap, unlike most of the rest of the Third World—one benefit of the revolution here.

People cope with all this in a variety of ways. To some extent, there's a real Me First mentality here. If you don't push and shove, you don't make it onto the buses. At the same time, paradoxically, there's also a real sense of people working together, selflessly, to overcome the problems that exist. When it became known last week at the University that the power was going to be shut off every afternoon for the next six weeks, the administration called an assembly to discuss and vote on the University's response. The administration was willing to shut

---

*This is equivalent to US $25, but the best way to understand salaries in any Third World country is to think of what they can buy, especially in terms of food.

down the school at 1:00 P.M. (without cuts in pay) if the employees were unwilling to work without electricity. But that wasn't what happened. I've never seen anything like it. One person after another stood up and spoke in favor of maintaining normal working hours, even without lights and air-conditioning, etc. They spoke in terms of a patriotic commitment to their work, with patriotism meaning "working together for the good of the country." "In response to the national emergency," they said, "We'll become *more* rather than less productive." Everybody was clapping and cheering.

I have to admit that I haven't seen any particular boost in productivity since then, and to some extent I think people were worried about losing their subsidized lunches if they went home early, but I was nonetheless impressed. Above all, I'm impressed by the real value that is placed on work here as a way to contribute to the betterment of society. And despite all the problems here, people still feel that, working together, they can bring about a better life for everybody. That's what the revolution means to them. Some of the people involved with the project where Peter works put in sixteen hour days entirely on their own initiative and without complaint because they believe in what they're doing. And I heard an older Nicaraguan woman speak to this issue at the US Embassy demonstration. She was a member of a base Christian community*, and had just come back from picking coffee in the mountains. (Coffee is Nicaragua's main source of foreign exchange.) "Every bean I pick," she said, "means another pill for some sick person in the hospital." This country is running on heart and guts and not much else. I hope they can keep it up.

And you all keep it up, on your end. Keep us in your

---

*The base Christian community movement started in the Latin American Catholic church in the 1960s. Such a community might consist of 10-30 people in a poor neighborhood or village, meeting regularly to study the Bible and reflect on how the Gospel applies to their daily lives. Community members help each other with their problems and often work together cooperatively to improve their surroundings, for example, by raising the money to bring piped water into their barrio. Base communities have been influenced by and in turn have influenced the theology of liberation. They have often been considered threatening by religious and secular power structures; however, the Sandinistas have encouraged them, and some say they have co-opted them.

thoughts and prayers, and don't let Reagan get away with it.

Again, I miss you all. Thanks to all of you who've helped us in any way.

Love,
Julia

LETTER TWO

Julia

It's a hot windy Sunday afternoon in Managua. I've been taking it easy all weekend, so I can be fresh and bright-eyed at 7:00 A.M. tomorrow when classes officially start at the School of Translation. Daily life here is made up of a series of crises, each of which makes the previous one appear unimportant. For example, the week before last I was tearing my hair out trying to round up the documentation I need for my contract. Then my passport got stolen and I had to deal with that. Then there was a brand-new threat of US invasion, which had everyone in a state of panic for several days. Monday, along with classes, I'll be back to dealing with my contract and my passport. I'm learning to take all this in my stride—it is, after all, an illusion of North American culture that one can have all aspects of life under control—but the cumulative effect is exhausting, and weekends are an important respite.

The economic situation has only gotten worse over the last couple months. In mid-February, as a way of combating inflation, the government changed over to a new currency system, in which 1000 old *cordobas* became worth one new *cordoba*, and everyone had to go to the bank to change their money. Before the change, we were grocery shopping with 50,000 and 100,000 *cordoba* notes. (The report in the *Washington Post* which claimed that people had to carry around huge bags full of cash in order to shop for food was just plain nonsense, by the way.) Another result of the change was that the official exchange rate for the dollar was set at ten to one, whereas before it was at 20,000 to one—thus cutting the buying power of the dollar in half and making life very expensive for tourists and volunteer workers here. At the same time, salaries, which are subject to government control, were quintupled to make up for some of the ground lost to the 1000% inflation last year. However, in a cost-cutting move and an attempt at greater efficiency, the government is laying off one third of its work-force, which means that with the strong Nicaraguan extended family, everyone who is getting a new higher salary will have to support any number of newly unemployed relatives.

Then, in order to really take on inflation, the government published an official price list for basic commodities, and announced that speculators who sold products above the official price would be prosecuted and fined. So far, none of this has had the desired result. When the government attempted to enforce the official price on beans and rice, private speculators pulled them off the market. Beans and rice, the two staples of diet here, are now only available "under the table" at prices six or seven times the official rate. Last week I got five pounds of beans for twenty-five *cordobas* a pound ($2.50 US) through a co-worker at the University, but I hear they're selling for up to forty *cordobas* now. A friend of ours who is staying with a poor family in the countryside told us that with beans and rice unavailable they're living on boiled green bananas with a tortilla now and then as a special treat. At Mass one Sunday in the church we go to, the priest, in an emotional homily, called upon any speculators in the congregation to stop "living on blood;" the Gospel reading had been about Jesus driving the profiteers from the temple.

Peter and I are still eating reasonably well. Eggs, milk, tortillas, fruit and vegetables are all available, and a few days ago I ran across soybeans for a reasonable price in the market (the Christian base communities are promoting soybean consump-tion, but other than that, there's not much demand for them). In general, however, shopping and cooking require a lot of creativity and energy, as you never know where you're going to find what and prices continue to rise at a frightening rate. In this atmosphere, the cost of food has become the main topic of conversation in all social settings. Several weeks ago, standing in line at the supermarket, I heard a little girl about three years old singing to herself, and what she was singing were the prices of things: "sixty, seventy, a hundred thousand...." She was far too young to understand numbers, but I'm sure that's all she hears from the adults around her.

Last week, however, worry about the economy was temporarily superseded by fear of war. Everyone had been looking forward with some hope to the upcoming cease-fire talks between the government and the *contras*, and then all of a sudden Reagan was accusing the Sandinistas of invading Honduras, and taking the opportunity to rush US troops into the region in preparation for a possible invasion of Nicaragua. None of the Nicaraguans I know denied that some Nicaraguan troops may have inadvertently crossed the border while fighting with the *contras* in the mountains near there, but I'm sure that by the time Reagan got done with the story it sounded like Soviet tanks were about to pour into Tegucigalpa.

In any case, Wednesday and Thursday last week were days of panic at the University. All the male teachers under forty were called to a meeting of their reserve battalion and told they might have to leave on Sunday—with classes starting Monday! Work came to a virtual standstill as we huddled around the radio and made nervous jokes about bombing raids. We were all laughing wildly at the small globe which hangs from the ceiling of our office, because if a bomb fell on the building "the whole world would come down on our heads!" Every three minutes the radio announcers would call out *Patria Libre o Morir* ("Free Homeland or Death") as if it were the call letters—which didn't make things any calmer.

Even when I tried to go about my business, feeling like an ostrich as I did so, it was hard to get anything done. I've been substitute-teaching for English classes which the University offers at the Central Bank, but those were cancelled on Thursday "because of the mobilization," and none of the teachers were told this till we actually got to the bank (telephone communication is always uncertain in Nicaragua). We were cursing Reagan all the way back to the University. As I was waiting at the bus stop, I saw graffiti that said "Yankee, we will not kneel down from hunger," and I was thinking that perhaps the US can't make Nicaragua kneel down, but they can certainly make this country hungry. They can disrupt daily life here on whim. Nicaragua has to take US threats seriously, and disrupt daily life in doing so, because one never knows when the threat might be serious. The US bombed Libya two years ago with very little excuse at all. It feels odd being a US citizen here under the circumstances, as if I've made myself a hostage by my own free will, but at least the Nicaraguans I work with appear to regard me as a fellow victim in the general panic. My government may be attacking their country, but they know I don't approve.

And by Friday, although the international situation hadn't gotten any better, at least it hadn't worsened. For whatever reason, everyone was calmer, and we managed to have a two hour staff meeting in which the war was only alluded to once: we decided to put off having the traditional beginning-of-semester party till things in the outside world look better.

I don't want to give the impression that life here is unrelievedly grim. Two weeks ago I took part in an immense parade in honor of International Women's Day, which ended up downtown in the Plaza of the Revolution. I was expecting a political rally with lots of speeches, but the tens of thousands of Nicaraguans present were really there to party. Before the speeches started, the loudspeakers were blaring dance music, *salsas* and *cumbias* with revolutionary lyrics. I ended up dancing one song after another with some wild old ladies in from the countryside. The Sandinista soldiers and police, both men and women, were out in full force, and they were all dancing with each other. Every few minutes another group of them would decide to make a human pyramid, climbing up on each other's shoulders with the red and black Sandinista flag on top. But the flag never stayed up for more than thirty seconds before they all toppled into the crowd around them, to the accompaniment of much laughter.

I got bored when Daniel Ortega insisted on talking for an hour, but the rest of the crowd didn't. They were all clapping and cheering and shouting spontaneous revolutionary slogans whenever he paused for breath. Then after the speeches a live band came on stage and played more dance music into the evening. But the biggest applause of all that afternoon was when the speaker from the Sandinista women's organization suggested that men should be helping with the housework—an idea whose time has come in Nicaragua. I think people continue to be devoted to the vision of the revolution because it's the only thing that gives them hope for a better future amidst all the day to day problems of life. And a day like International Women's Day gives people a chance to celebrate their hope for the future.

I wanted to write more about the Church here, and about the University where I'm working, but I think I'll save that for another newsletter. Before I close, I should say that Peter's work is going well. Despite a lot of health and other problems, including a burst appendix and a truck accident, the Seattle Construction Brigade made a good start on the dormitory and kitchen buildings for the school, and now that they're gone, Peter is continuing to work with a crew of five Nicaraguans. This is challenging to his Spanish, but a good experience for him. The work involves a lot of digging trenches, moving around precast cement columns by hand and mixing cement in wheelbarrows, but they're well on the way to getting the wall structure done on both buildings. The crew works from 7:00 A.M. to 4:00 P.M. and they're surprised that Peter takes Saturday off. "What do you do? Drink all day?" they ask. But Peter has an hour commute each way, which they don't have. Unfortunately, the project is about to run out of material funds, especially at the current exchange rate, but the rainy season starts in May anyway, after which Peter will probably be working more directly with the disabled kids.

Meanwhile, our living situation continues to be comfortable, our health continues to be good, and despite all the problems, we're happy to be in Nicaragua. At least one thing has improved since we've been here—the Spanish and the Argentineans recently donated some buses to the Managua fleet, so transportation is much easier than it was when we first arrived. If only the US would do the same!

The mail is unreliable, but we have gotten some letters since we've been here, and we really, really appreciate them. We look forward to hearing from all of you!

And please keep us in your thoughts and prayers.

Lots of love,
Julia

LETTER THREE

Julia

We're just on the verge of the rainy season here, which means that it's hotter and more humid than ever. They say that once the rains start it's cooler. Even the Nicaraguans are complaining about the weather and asking each other "when is it going to rain?' Weather like this makes people nervous, because there's a popular belief that particularly hot, muggy days are the sign of a coming earthquake. Three times in the last month our landlady, Doña Fide, has said "Either it's going to rain or there's going to be an earthquake." And each time she's been right—we've had one rainstorm and two *temblors* which have frightened people without causing damage.

The good news is that I finally got paid last week—one big check for the three months I'd been working at the UCA. We went out to dinner to celebrate and spent more on one meal than some Nicaraguans make in a month. This weekend I've been doing my Christmas shopping and stocking up on things like beans, vinegar and shampoo. After living such an austere existence for so long, I feel uncomfortable spending so much so fast, but it doesn't do any good at all to save money here with prices going up so fast. The worst of the food shortages are over, but that's only because the government has given up on enforcing price controls. "A victory for free enterprise," Peter commented. The only thing that hasn't gone up is the price of milk, and that's only because the government is subsidizing its cost with the price of cheese, which has risen dramatically.

The cease-fire is still in effect, which is giving people in the countryside a breathing space. However, it'll be over by the end of May unless the Sandinistas and the *contras* can agree on extending it, which so far they haven't been able to do. When the cease-fire first started there was a lot of hope that peace might really be at hand, but that hope has receded somewhat since the negotiations haven't gotten anywhere. The mood was very ambiguous last month when the *contra* delegation first came to town to negotiate. On the one hand this was something new that had never been tried before and which might end the war. On the other hand, a lot of people who have had relatives killed really hate the *contras*, and they were angered by their presence in Managua. A lot of them wanted to demonstrate right in front of the hotel where the *contra* leaders were staying, out on the highway near the airport, and they did in fact carry on a round-the-clock vigil while the negotiations were going on, but the Sandinista police wouldn't let the demonstrators closer than one kilometer from the hotel because they didn't want any incidents occurring that could hurt the Sandinista position.

Meanwhile, the Mothers of the Heroes and Martyrs, an association of those who have had family members killed or kidnapped by the *contras*, were demanding that the Sandinistas not release from prison any more ex-National Guardsmen until the *contras* account for all those they've taken. Daniel Ortega picked up the Mothers' demand in a speech he gave, pointing out that the mothers of the jailed Somocistas can at least visit their sons in prison, while those who have had children kidnapped by the *contras* don't even know if they are alive or dead.

The ex-National Guardsmen, convicted by revolutionary tribunals of torture and murder, are being released gradually over a long period of time to meet the demands of the US State Department, which refers to them as political prisoners. Their re-entry into society has exacerbated fears of crime in the streets here. As Doña Fide says, looking as if the whole thing gives her a headache, "They don't have any money and they don't have any work, so of course they're going to turn to crime." Whether the Somocistas, who were certainly involved in crime before the revolution, are contributing to the current crime wave is a matter for conjecture, but it is true that Managua, which a few years ago was considered "very safe," is now so no longer. There have been a number of armed robberies in our neighborhood, and at least two recent murders. Our landlady's maid, Socorrito, was held up at knife-point at a bus stop in broad daylight, and a few days later her sister was assaulted by two men who took her entire month's salary. There's also a lot of pickpocketing and bag-slashing on the crowded buses by thieves going after wallets. All of this contributes to the atmosphere of suspicion in a city that's already tense and politically polarized.

The union mechanics and construction workers have been on strike since the big money change-over in February when new wage-levels were set by the Sandinistas. Apparently the salary board (acronym S.N.O.T.S.) decided that they had been making too much money (four-five times what university professors were getting), and at a time when everyone else was getting pay raises to keep up with inflation, these people were cut back to about a fourth of what they had been making, with no differential for skills or experience. They were understandably furious. The Sandinistas have so far refused to negotiate and have been calling the strikers "deserters from the work front." It's true that there's very little money and resources to go around, and that one of the few things that could alleviate the economic crisis would be increased production. It's also widely believed that the strike is being directed, or at least manipulated, by the US Embassy, which is poised to exploit any rifts in this society to the utmost, and which certainly has the resources to do so.

In any case, a couple weeks ago the union members began a hunger strike (the pro-government newspapers have been publishing lists of the food they say is being smuggled into them), and on May Day (I think) there was some kind of clash between the strikers and the police, which ended with the arrests of a number of the strike leaders. The right-wing radio stations had a field day, spreading rumors that one of the men arrested had been beaten to death in jail, and claiming that this was an example of the "Nazi-like" tactics of the brutal Sandinistas. This story lasted until the alleged corpse appeared live on Sandinista TV, without a visible scratch, to say that the rumors of his death had been greatly exaggerated. Now it was the turn of the left-wing press to have the last laugh: they called this "the case of the living dead." And the government shut down the morning news programs on the right-wing radio stations for a week in retaliation. With all of this, the whole situation has really degenerated into name-calling, and I think it's time for the Sandinistas (one of whose new slogans is "We are flexible, because the revolution is strong") to admit they've made some mistakes and at least negotiate with the strikers, even if the new wages they are demanding are ridiculously high. A lot of people around the University, who are normally Sandinista sympathizers, have at least some sympathy for the strikers. At any rate, this situation is a sign that the Sandinistas can't take the working class for granted any more.

This is also a symptom of the problem known as *burocratismo*. Although this country is supposedly based on "power to the people," and to some extent this is true, a lot of the decisions that affect people's lives (such as the one about salary levels) are made by faceless bureaucrats. This wouldn't be so bad except that a lot of the bureaucrats are not in their positions because they are competent, knowledgeable and hard-working, but rather because they have political connections: either they fought in the insurrection or they know someone who did. This is a country where some people take long lunch breaks and other people wait in line for them to come back.

This phenomenon, I know, goes far beyond the borders of Nicaragua. Most people in the world are at the mercy of some bureaucracy or other, and many bureaucracies are inefficient. It should be noted, moreover, that in this country such jobs don't pay very well. You can make more money selling coca-cola on the street than you can working for the government. However, in Nicaragua the economy is so fragile due to the war and the US trade embargo that there's no margin for error—one small mistake and people go hungry. A woman I know who is an economist for the Ministry of Agriculture told me that, in her opinion, the ministry brought the rice and beans shortage on themselves because of glitches in the food distribution system, with the problem of speculation being incidental to this. Another example, of course, is the fact that it took my first paycheck three months to clear all the red tape. And recently an employee of the government telephone company (TELCOR) typed some wrong information into the computer and cut off one eighth of the phones in Managua. And although the phone company has acknowledged its error, it's still requiring those who have been cut off to come into the office and pay a sizable reconnection fee. (One of my co-workers sighed and said "If the *contras* have to assassinate someone, why don't they assassinate the head of TELCOR?")

The Sandinista government, on their part, recognizes that all of this bureaucratic inefficiency is a serious problem. And with their usual dramatic flair, they have laid off one third of all government employees as a way of encouraging efficiency in those who remain. In the long run it's probably a good move. In the short run, I'm sure it's contributed to things like the phone fiasco. I fear that many of those who have been laid off are not those who were incompetent, but rather those whose political connections were not good enough.

Nevertheless, this country continues to lurch forward into the future. The electricity hasn't been cut off for several weeks, and there've been fewer hours of water-rationing since some new wells came on line. Some things get better as others get worse. The Sandinistas have set an impossibly high ideal of self-sacrifice and dedication for themselves. Although they continue struggling to achieve this ideal, they often fail to live up to it—leading to cries that they are "betraying the revolution." Does this mean that the ideal should be abandoned? I don't think so.

The Nicaraguan Church is in the middle of all the struggles in the society here. When North Americans come down here for a week, they often end up going to Mass at the Church of Maria de Los Angeles, which has beautiful revolutionary murals all over the walls and a professional-quality Latin American folk band singing the *misa campesina*. They chant revolutionary slogans during the services, and the pastor makes "the best political speeches in town, next to Tomas Borge*," says a friend of ours. In many ways it's a wonderful experience to be there as the whole building rocks with passionate religious and political conviction—however, the problem is that a lot of people go

---

*Minister of the Interior and only surviving founder of the Sandinista movement.

back to the US thinking that this is "the Church in Nicaragua" or even "the Church in Latin America."

As a matter of fact, Maria de los Angeles is unique in the world. And the Nicaraguan Church is a Church divided. On the one hand you have the bourgeois churches with perfect sound systems and parking lots full of nice cars, where the parishioners think that the Sandinistas are godless Communists. On the other hand you've got the little cement block chapels of the base communities in the barrios, where the music (if any) is a couple of teenagers on battered guitars, and where tough-looking old women sell fruit drinks after Mass to raise money to buy sewing machines for the community.

One base community we visited had invited Cardinal Obando (back when he was an Archbishop) to bless their chapel, but when he saw that it had a dirt floor he wouldn't even get out of his car. Even worse, a priest we know told us that in one of the dioceses up north the bishop has fired all the volunteer catechists who have been working there for fifteen years because he thinks they're too involved with the Sandinistas. New catechists are now being trained by the diocese, but the old catechists are not eligible for the training programs.

All of this creates great confusion in the minds of the faithful.

We've mostly been attending Mass in a small church with tacky plaster statues in a working class neighborhood not far from where we live. It's a regular parish, not a base community, but because the Spanish Dominican fathers who work there are supportive of the "revolutionary process," they're in conflict with the church hierarchy, and the parish has lost members because of this. Supporting the revolutionary process means encouraging people to take part in government-sponsored vaccination campaigns and neighborhood clean-up days, and in general believing that Christians have a responsibility to work together to bring about the kingdom of God "on earth as it is in heaven," as Jesus said. We frequently go to the 9:00 A.M. children's Mass there, where ten year olds do the scripture readings and four year olds come trotting up to the scratchy microphone to pray for peace.

I've written far too much again, and haven't even begun to

talk about my work, which I'm enjoying. I shall let Peter talk about his work this time, and write a wrap-up of my first semester at the UCA in my next effort. Please keep writing to us. We miss you all, and we love getting mail. Some things get lost and other things take six weeks, but many letters have gotten through. If you write to us, we'll write to you.

Lots of love,
Julia

Peter

Over three months have passed since our arrival here in Nicaragua. So far the experience has been satisfying, frustrating, empowering, humbling and much more. For me it has been a very full and busy time; only recently do I feel confident enough with my situation to attempt writing about it in detail.

The Hans Gutiérrez Cooperative, where I work, is a new school and small farm project for developmentally disabled children and young adults. It is situated on forty-five acres of land just outside Ciudad Sandino, about ten miles from Managua. The cooperative was formed through the efforts of the students' parents and Frances Romero, a special education teacher from the US, who moved to Nicaragua five years ago. As a developing country, Nicaragua had only low-level special education programs, and nothing for the students after age thirteen. The need was obvious for an on-going and more stimulating environment, so the parents organized and petitioned the Sandinista government for aid. The government here is virtually bankrupt. They cannot afford to fund new projects, but did provide the land through the agrarian reform program and guaranteed that the project would get priority in terms of building materials being available. At the time the land was offered there was neither sufficient personnel or funding to take on such a project. The idea was to start with a lower-key school program in Managua. However, it was urgent to start something, so the offer of land was accepted, and the project went ahead on the faith that staff and funding needs would be met.

When I arrived in January, the students were on Christmas break, which is equal in length to summer vacation in the States. One small house had already been built on the land; this is currently being used for many purposes including tool storage, classroom space, caretaker's quarters, kitchen and, most important, a place to take refuge from the sun. The first crop of beans, tomatoes and *pipian* squash was mostly a failure due to over-enthusiasm during planting and not enough rain. The second crop of sorghum was a success thanks to the help of workers and equipment from a nearby state farm. Part of the agreement upon receiving the land was that it would be agriculturally productive. This will be easier in the future when a well is drilled on the site. For now, the one crop a year is dependent on the rains, and all domestic water is hauled to the site in a water tank trailer behind the jeep. A construction brigade from Seattle also came in January. During their five week stay, two other buildings were started, the dining hall and a dormitory.

My role is in the hands-on construction end of the project. I worked with the brigade from Seattle and have continued on with a crew of four Nicaraguans from Ciudad Sandino. The slow pace of accomplishing anything in Nicaragua can be frustrating at times. We are building on a site that is only accessible over bumpy dirt roads and has no electricity, so the work is done with hand tools, muscle and sweat. The walls of the buildings are constructed using a system of precast concrete columns and slabs that fit into grooves in the sides of the columns. All the cement for the column pedestals and connecting beams at the top and bottom of the walls is mixed by hand and moved to the forms in wheelbarrows and buckets. All the digging for the footings had to be done by hand as well. The few cement mixers and backhoes in Nicaragua are kept busy on bigger projects. Keep in mind that this construction site is out on the edge of some flat sorghum fields with no shade trees and temperatures often pushing 100 degrees with high humidity. I often dunk my hat in the water barrel and put it back on wet to gain from the evaporative cooling effect. In the States, three months would be enough to complete two buildings of this size.

At the Gutiérrez site all we have done is the perimeter walls up to top beam where they are ready for roofs. Quite a difference, but there is satisfaction in looking at those walls and having an intimate relationship with almost every column and slab. The columns weigh over 200 lbs a piece and the slabs about 120 lbs, so they are not easy to ignore while moving them into place.

A real source of joy for me has been daily contact with the working-class Nicaraguans on the crew. These are men from Ciudad Sandino with varying skill levels but big hearts and a willingness to work. They were accepting of me from the start and are very patient with my constant questions about Spanish grammar, vocabulary and pronunciation. None of them speak English, so out of necessity my Spanish has improved quickly. I have even attempted some political discussions over lunch or during breaks in the little shade that is available. At mid-day this means standing under the scaffold boards because they are the only thing casting a shadow.

I have learned a lot from my Nicaraguan co-workers. Their experience comes from a lifetime of manual labor, often without the aid of electricity or other types of power that North American tradespeople are so dependent on. The little tricks they know for hand-mixing cement a certain way or moving a heavy object are things I never think about when I have a machine or a special tool to do the job.

Misael, who helped keep the job running smoothly, is a carpenter and mason. Just watching him work was an education. He knows exactly how to sharpen and set the teeth on a hand saw to rip the length of a twelve-foot board with the least amount of effort. He often engaged me in conversation during siesta; curious about the English language, he would watch the way my mouth moved and then practice over and over until he had it. He wanted to know about the North American way of life and was a little shocked when I talked about homeless people and unemployment in the United States. Construction work at the Gutiérrez site has had to stop for a while due to a lack of funds, so Misael is off on another job already. I will miss him.

Vidal, at fifty-two, is the senior citizen on the crew. He is known in the area as the *viejito malcriado* (the "ill-bred little old man"), because he is stubborn and opinionated—but aren't we all? I have never had a problem with him and he puts me to shame when it comes to hard work.

Paulino, the youngest and most out-going, has become a good friend. He is the one I usually have my lunch-time discussions with, while the others offer comments and clarification. Paulino was drafted into the army to fight against the *contras*. Given only eight days training, he was sent into combat, where due to erratic supply deliveries, he at times had to go as long as seven or eight days without food. He served his time but didn't care for the experience. He thinks the Servicio Militar Patriotico Law is unjust in requiring all men of draft age to serve with little concern for their circumstances. His wife and young son were left alone when he was called up, and his cousins who are responsible for daily operation of the family farm were called at the same time, leaving only wives and small children to do the work. I pointed out that many countries have military conscription even in peacetime. Paulino and Vidal are quick to criticize the Sandinistas and blame them for all of Nicaragua's problems, but this is somewhat due to an uninformed viewpoint. When I talk about the United States supplying the *contras* and imposing the trade embargo, they agree that this is causing problems beyond the Sandinistas' control. I had lunch with Paulino in Ciudad Sandino the other day, and was able to meet his *señora*, his mother and his two little boys. He appears to be as kind and gentle at home as he is at work.

Rounding out the crew is Walter, one of the older, higher-functioning boys in the school program. He walks every day from his house in Ciudad Sandino to the work site, about a mile through the fields. Walter is big, strong and very helpful around the construction site. His main disability is with his speech, complicated by a slight hearing defect. The Gutiérrez project is to be a residential school where the students live during the week and spend weekends with their families in Managua and Ciudad Sandino. Walter understands this, and is excited about helping to build "his school."

Now that construction has stopped for a while, I will be changing hats and working more with the students. For the next two weeks, I will work with Walter and Jose Luis, another boy from Ciudad Sandino. We will be doing various maintenance jobs, like fence-mending, brush-cutting, hand-watering the *platano* trees, and organizing the tool room. Once the regular classes start on May 23 for the whole group I will be part-time bus driver and part-time teacher's aide for the students, who will be going to the cooperative four days a week. I have enjoyed working on the construction but look forward to a change from the back-breaking labor and a chance to get to know the students better.

Over-all I am quite pleased with how our time here is going. Managua is a hot, crowded, dirty Central American city, but it is a much more livable place than I imagined before moving here. I haven't been doing much running since our arrival, but I bicycle at least five miles a day, and when I take the bus to work, I walk the two miles round-trip from Ciudad Sandino. I'm hoping my new schedule will allow me to take some runs in the early morning when it is cool.

This is the first time I have had a good bicycle to use for transportation. It makes getting around Managua a lot easier. At times it can't be beat, like when I'm coasting down the long hill from the Romeros in the late afternoon with a grand view of the sun setting into the hills to the west. This same route also takes me past the US Embassy, which is more fortified than the Sandinista military bases in town. The other night we saw the Canadian folk-singer, Bruce Cockburn, who has a song about Nicaragua written after his first trip here. The line referring to this same Embassy drips with truth: "looming over town like Dracula's castle."

Now that Julia is getting paid, our new-found wealth should allow us to take some trips to other parts of Nicaragua. Thus far I have only gone on a couple short outings. One was just for the day, down to Casares, a fishing village and beach on the Pacific coast south of here. The other trip was to Santo Tomas, a hundred miles east of Managua, to see friends working on a construction brigade from Olympia, Washington. It was interesting to visit an area more directly affected by the war. The contras had recently attacked the military post on the edge of town and had burned some buses, reportedly once with some of the passengers inside. People were relieved during the week I was there to see the cease-fire go into effect. There are some other projects in the countryside I want to visit, so let's hope the cease-fire holds. Julia and I plan to go to Matagalpa up in the hills next weekend for a little vacation and a break from the heat. We have one fan in our room that we take turns sitting in front of.

I hope this provides a picture of what I have been up to. My only regret: that it's May, the Boston Celtics are in the playoffs, and I can't watch Larry Bird cut outside, grab a pass, throw a head-fake, and toss in a shot with icy precision. The Romeros get the *New York Times*, so at least I can read the box scores.

En la lucha,
Peter

Images of Nicaragua: a boy in Ciudad Sandino pushing a home-made wooden cart with a chrome Mercedes-Benz emblem nailed to the front. Cowboys, horses, cattle in the main street.

LETTER FOUR

Julia

MANAGUA, NICARAGUA
July 5, 1988

The rainy season started about seven weeks ago, transforming the countryside—which was a relief to the farmers after last year's drought. Within a few days everything had turned a lush, vibrant green, and the grass has been growing about an inch a day. The cows, pigs, goats and horses that graze on the vacant lots of Managua are looking fat and happy. Around the time the rains started, the big spreading *malinche* trees burst into brilliant red blossoms, which are only now beginning to fall. It doesn't rain every day, and it rarely rains all day long, but when it does rain it tends to come down in torrents, accompanied by spectacular thunder and lightning. The rainy season also means rats, mice, flies and fleas, but when the rain stops it's so miserably hot that I'm always happy to see the clouds rolling in again.

In terms of the war—it hasn't really heated up again since the cease-fire ended. We haven't heard of any direct clashes between Sandinistas and *contra* troops, and although the Sandinistas are drafting a lot of men, they've said they won't be the ones to fire the first shot. On the other hand, there have been some hit-and-run *contra* attacks on non-military targets: agricultural cooperatives and civilian vehicles in the back country. Even during the official cease-fire period the *contras* never really stopped kidnapping *campesinos*; we've heard that as many as several hundred people may have been kidnapped during this period of so-called "peace." Most of those who are kidnapped are never heard from again—those who have escaped have said that men are typically given the choice between death and joining the *contra* forces, while women have to choose between gang-rape and accepting the "protection" of an individual *contra*

35

soldier. The *contras* recently released seventy people amidst a lot of hoopla, but there are still thousands unaccounted for.

In terms of the economy—in the middle of June the Sandinistas dropped a lot of the economic measures they'd adopted in February because they didn't seem to be having the desired effect on inflation. The official value of the dollar rose overnight from 13-1 to 130-1 (now it's at 200-1). The government also removed its few remaining subsidies from food items and announced that it would no longer attempt to enforce any price controls. We're on the free market system now, and I think a lot of people who were complaining about socialism are seeing that the alternative is no better. Prices of all imported goods, such as gasoline and medicine, immediately jumped 8-10 times. The price of rice has tripled in three weeks, and most other food items have followed suit. Meanwhile salaries have gone up 30%, but they are still woefully inadequate. If you can imagine $75-a-pound rice and $60-a-dozen eggs, you can imagine what grocery shopping is like for people at the lower end of the salary scale, who take home 1500 *cordobas* (or often less) a month, and have to pay 150 *cordobas* a pound for rice. I really don't know how people are surviving; a lot of people must be going hungry. My salary is better than most people's, but we may have to change some dollars to make it through to the next pay check. One of my co-workers, who also makes a professor's salary, is threatening to quit her job and go to work selling tamales with her mother-in-law....

But enough bad news. For the rest of the newsletter I'm going to talk about my job.

The first semester at the Universidad Centroamericana will be over by the time you receive this. I've been teaching in the School of Translation, a professional training program which takes kids right out of the abysmal high school English program here and attempts to produce competent bilinguals at the end of five years. It's a tough program and many of the students who sign up for it fall by the wayside. This year we will graduate our first class of about twelve students. There is, we understand, a big demand for translators by the government ministries here, both to provide access to English language technical material and to shepherd the innumerable delegations of foreigners who come here to find out about the Revolution. Our hope is that our students *will* stay in Nicaragua and put their skills to use in service to their homeland, but we know that, realistically, a number of graduates will head for the United States or Costa Rica, like so many other Nicaraguan professionals before them.

I have exclusively been teaching the sixteen students who make up the third year of the program. Only two of them are male, which is a common phenomenon in Nicaraguan universities these days. So many of the young men are either in the army or dead that the next generation of professionals is going to be female.

In general, my students are an uninhibited lot, like most Nicaraguans, ready to complain loudly if they feel put upon, and equally ready to have a good time if the occasion presents itself. I always have plenty of feedback on my teaching. Moreover, because they've been taking all of the same classes together for two and a half years now, they all know each other very well and enjoy cooperating on group projects.

Most of my students were in junior high school at the time of the revolutionary triumph in 1979, so they were too young to fight in the insurrection themselves—but many have vivid memories of the National Guard lobbing tear-gas into their classrooms, or of wounded street fighters seeking refuge in their homes. Since then, the continuing process of the revolution has shaped their experiences. A number of them, at age fourteen or fifteen, took part in the 1980 Literacy Campaign, an experience which involved five months of living with *campesino* families, working in their fields and teaching them to read—a very different way of life from the middle-class existence they'd been accustomed to. Since that time they've taken part in coffee-picking brigades and vaccination campaigns, while the two young men in the group have both done their obligatory military service in the war against the *contras*. As one of the classes I teach is English composition, and as I encourage them to write about their own lives, I am able to read about all this in the short essays they turn in every week—a fringe benefit of teaching.

Given the fact that so many of my students are women, it's not too surprising that feminism is an issue that has come up over and over again. It first surfaced when, in the course of illustrating some otherwise unrelated topic, I asked the class to give me a few reasons for getting a divorce. Within three minutes the blackboard was entirely covered with variations on a theme—that Nicaraguan men are macho, irresponsible, and just plain no-good. They drink, they hit you, they run around with other women, they expect to be waited on. The men in the class tried to defend themselves, but they were clearly outnumbered. The women are good-humoured and not bitter about it all, but they do agree that most of the revolutionary rhetoric about the New Man and the New Woman has been no more than lip-service, and that women who want to make their own way in this world still have to struggle constantly against macho ideas. The men in the class agree with the liberation of women in the abstract, and admire people like Nora Astorga (who was Ambassador to the United Nations before she died of cancer), but they're not quite ready yet to take on an equal share of the housework.

There's quite a bit more disagreement in the class over some of the other social and political issues which are so controversial in this country. As far as I can tell, they all feel that such goals of the revolution as universal health care and education are worthwhile and important, and also that the US-backed aggression is a crime. "Reagan is as bad as Hitler. We will never forget what he's done to us," a couple of them told me one day, and nobody disagreed with them. However, they differ widely in terms of their personal commitment towards helping the revolution achieve its goals, and also in how much they respect the Sandinistas. A number of them feel that the present government is corrupt and incompetent: "Daniel Ortega has a nice car and a nice house and he gets to travel to Europe, while we have a hard time buying food to eat." They think, moreover, that the Sandinistas should end the military service and allow an opposition TV station—but it's the economic issues that really cut to the bone.

I have noticed, however, that the students who make these kinds of criticisms the loudest are the ones whose outlook on life is essentially selfish: *they* want a nice car and a nice house, and the rest of society can get along by itself. The ones who have a personal commitment to making life better for everybody tend to back the Sandinistas wholeheartedly. Political issues come up over and over again, in debates, in role-plays, in the oral reports that students have to present three times a semester. I've made it a policy to encourage this kind of exchange, and I've never noticed anyone hesitate to speak her mind, often at the top of her lungs and in language that could be considered insulting. (If anyone reading this seriously thinks that Nicaragua is a repressive society, let me point out that one of my students works for the Sandinista Police and another for the Ministry of the Interior, but that their presence does not seem to put a damper on the debate.) Moreover, I've never noticed students becoming resentful of each other personally, even when the political comments conflict with their own deeply cherished ideals. Friends can apparently disagree markedly on the future of Nicaragua and still remain close.

Probably the most interesting thing we did all semester was also the most political: I designed a role-play based on the continuing and highly controversial construction workers and mechanics strike, described in our last newsletter, in which they have demanded that the government salary board assign them to a higher pay scale. I assigned different students to play strikers, Sandinistas, CIA agents, opposition journalists, etc.; the goal was to settle the strike before the end of class. Although the students who were playing the Sandinistas (some of them against their real political convictions) attempted to negotiate in good faith, and indeed made beautiful speeches about coopera-tion and working together to solve the economic crisis, those playing the strikers were gleefully scribbling inflammatory slogans on sheets of paper and tacking them on the walls ("The Sandinistas have stolen more in nine years than Somoza did in forty"), and entirely refusing to listen. When I asked them why they'd refused to negotiate, they airily replied "Oh, the US Embassy is giving us money, so we don't need to go back to work." How closely these kinds of role-plays reflect life in Managua is an open question, but they keep me interested, and they certainly provide excellent practice in speaking English.

In any case, life in Managua is hard and slowly getting harder for everyone—and translation students are no exception.

They're in class six hours a day, they're required to put in 100 hours of social service in their field every semester, many of them face long commutes on unreliable buses, some of them have children and a number of them have jobs. Moreover, there are rumors flying, probably false, that tuition is sky-rocketing next semester, far beyond the rate of inflation. Not one but two compositions last week were about struggling with the decision to drop out of school for economic reasons. These students have worked long and hard to become professionals and it would be a shame to give up that dream, but when you can't afford to buy notebooks and your younger brothers and sisters are going hungry, present needs begin to take priority. Existence is precarious here, and sometimes it takes a real act of faith to believe that things will be better in the future.

Before I finish, I'd like to give brief portraits of some of my more memorable students:

Rosa is my most dedicated Sandinista. Utterly committed to making the revolution work, "it's a moral commitment to improve society," she exhausts herself working full time for the Ministry of the Interior and caring for her severely retarded daughter.

Juan and Cinthia, boyfriend and girlfriend, commute together from Masaya every day, which means catching a bus at 5:00 A.M. to be in class by 7:00. They have not been late or absent once, and they have never missed a homework assignment. They sit together in the back of class and are usually very quiet, but Juan writes really funny compositions about screw-ups that happened when he was in the military.

Vicky is a cheerful and assertive young woman who comes from León. She works in her mother's flower shop on weekends and is engaged to marry a doctor. Her dream, however, is to move to the States, where her father has lived for the last ten years.

Diego, a young Sandinista police officer, works nights on foot patrol in poor neighborhoods with high crime rates. He is married with two small children who keep him awake in the few hours he has for sleep—when he dozes off in class, I try to be understanding. A number of the female students have crushes on him, which doesn't seem to bother him too much.

Fanny, from Matagalpa, always beautifully dressed, projects an aura of being a spoiled little rich girl, but she's good-hearted and she has a sense of humor, so she's not too intolerable. She complains louder than anyone in the class when the textbooks are boring or when she thinks I'm giving too much homework. She's a great story-teller, but the more she worries about the economic and political situation, the worse her grammar gets.

Carmen, in her early thirties, is the oldest student in the class. She was a union organizer when she was younger and now feels bad to be "just a housewife" (even though she's in school full time). Her husband has worked for the diplomatic service, so she's lived in Sweden and the Dutch Antilles. Responsible for both her own children and her husband's teenagers, she arrives late more often than anyone in the class and is constantly forgetting to do her homework.

Finally, I'd just like to say that although the *contra* leaders in Miami can drag their feet indefinitely about coming back to the negotiating table and the US Congress can, without any inconvenience to themselves, continue the trade embargo forever—nevertheless, people here have waited for peace long enough! There's no hope of slowing inflation as long as the war continues, and we're starting to hear about people fainting in streets from hunger. As Rosa said to me after class one day, "All we can hope for now is that we will be able to buy food. We can't even think about buying clothes for the children." I'm going to be teaching "English Composition III" to these same students next semester, and I'm looking forward to continuing my relationship with them—but I'm very much afraid some of them won't be there. It's not right that decisions made in the United States should have so much power over their lives!

As you can see, teaching here has meant a lot to me, and it's a good thing, because I'm still not reconciled to the heat and the humidity, and although the endless petty problems involved in eking out an existence here no longer drive me into a state of panic, let me just say that grocery shopping is no fun. But Peter and I are glad to be here, we're enjoying each other's company (approaching our sixth anniversary), and actually our biggest hardship is missing all of you. We've been very faithful about letter-writing, and we guarantee that if you write to us (and your letter is not lost in the mail), we will write back to you promptly. We *love* getting letters. Please don't hesitate any longer, those of you deadbeats who haven't written at all. And those of you who have written—thanks again.

Take care. Do what you can for peace. Enjoy your summer.

Lots of love,
Julia

Peter

My view of Managua these last two months has mostly been from behind the wheel of a car. This is partly because there has been no construction going on out at the cooperative but also due to a lack of drivers on the staff. A big problem here is that many Nicaraguans don't drive and the hired chauffeurs who do it for a living tend to be an irresponsible lot. After going through a succession of these hired drivers, the decision was made to try and get along without them.

Although I don't enjoy the driving, at least it has meant more contact with the retarded young people we are trying to help. I have really enjoyed getting to know them better. Two days a week we are taking small groups of them down to Rivas, near the Costa Rican border, where a couple of young dentists are willing to donate their services. The dental supplies were donated by a group in the States, and as a result our students are able to get some dental work done that wouldn't have happened otherwise. I spent last Wednesday afternoon with Oscar, a Downs Syndrome boy who refused to cooperate with the dentist. He couldn't believe all the ripe mangoes dropping off the trees as we walked and must have eaten six or eight of them, probably creating a terrible case of diarrhea the next day.

There is another brigade coming down to help, this time from Marin County, California. I am already figuring up the necessary materials from the plans and will be running around trying to buy and transport them to the work site. This is a challenge because the materials are expensive when you can find them and the roads into the cooperative are in terrible shape due to the rains. I prefer to go in on foot like most of the people who work out in that area, but it's tough to transport sand, gravel and sacks of cement that way.

I'm excited about this next phase of the construction and look forward to working more with Walter and Jose Luis. It does wonders for all of us when we spend a day together out at the cooperative. So you can see I'm keeping busy even when I am a little out of my element.

With love,
Peter

MANAGUA, NICARAGUA
July 13, 1988

No sooner had we mailed off our newsletter last week, when there were any number of exciting and distressing political developments here. And with what we've heard about how these are being reported in the US press, we didn't want to wait a couple months before sending you the other side of the story.

In any case, on Sunday the 10th the right-wing opposition political parties held a march in the small town of Nandaime, south of Managua. Apparently, the US press is reporting that there were 40,000 there. The Nicaraguan media is saying 2000. We also understand that the US press is reporting police brutality. However, television news footage here showed the demonstrators wielding knives and large clubs, and uniformed police officers being carried away on stretchers. Ten of them ended up in the hospital. Demonstrators were arrested, but I don't think any of them were injured, at least not badly. They were, however, repelled with tear gas. What *exactly* happened at Nandaime is probably impossible to determine. It does seem clear, though, that the event was organized by the US Embassy in the hopes of provoking an incident which could be used to sell more *contra* aid. Embassy staff were at the demonstration "directing things," it is said. They also provided transportation there from Managua. It doesn't do the Sandinistas any good to create an international flap like this, and they wouldn't have expelled Ambassador Melton if his behavior hadn't been outrageous. Nicaragua needs opposition political parties which are responsible, independent, constructive and principled—but this is not the direction they're getting pushed by the Embassy. (For this reason, US aid to the opposition parties, now very popular in Congress, should be opposed.) It's one thing to have a demonstration; it's another thing to beat on the police with large clubs. I should also mention that *La Prensa** and *Radio Catolica*, now closed temporarily by the Sandinistas, have been paid large amounts of money by the Embassy to report their version of events.

Meanwhile, the *contras* have really stepped up their attacks on vehicles traveling in remote areas. The attached photograph is of a sixteen year old girl, Giovana Zavala, who was machine-gunned by the *contras*. From what it said in the newspaper, she was on her way to visit a military camp outside Rio Blanco in north-central Nicaragua, along with her boyfriend's military dance troupe and a number of relatives of young draftees stationed at the camp. The *contras* stopped the truck with a land mine and then opened fire. Giovana, another teen-age girl, and a forty-five year old woman were killed outright. Giovana's boyfriend, Miguel Guevara, could have escaped (they say), but he came back to help her and was kidnapped, tortured with a knife, and then murdered, along with another member of the dance troupe.

This and similar events are the other reason why Ambassador Melton was expelled from Nicaragua. A number of the *contra* leaders were in favor of a negotiated settlement with the Sandinistas, but the US chose to back Enrique Bermúdez, who wanted to continue the war. And so the war continues. The *contras* can't win, but they can continue murdering and torturing civilians while their Miami leadership draws large salaries. I'm sending you Giovana's picture because it's doubtful that it will ever appear in a US newspaper.

Peace,
Julia

---

*The opposition newspaper

LETTER SIX

Julia

The rainy season continues. It's been one of the wettest years on record. Apparently the flood damage to the crops this year is equal to the drought damage last year. Peter experienced this at first hand when he was trapped on the wrong side of a drainage ditch for an hour and a half by a flash flood. Socorrito, the maid in our house, tells us that at her family farm in the hills outside Granada all the beans have been wiped out and the corn is infested with insects. At least the rice crop is happy, but most of the rice growers are big land-owners. It's the small farmers and the consumers that are going to suffer.

The austerity measures that the Sandinistas put in place in June finally managed to slow inflation. They held down salaries to the point where a significant number of people couldn't afford to buy anything, so the price of beans and rice actually remained steady for almost two months. Then to keep public employees from starving, the government has been handing out ten pounds of beans, ten of rice and five of sugar along with each monthly pay-check—a popular move. If I tell you that the food they gave me in August was worth over a third of my check, you will see how low the salaries have been. However, in September salaries will be boosted 140%. The government-controlled prices of milk and gasoline have recently doubled, and the price of beans and rice in the market has followed suit. At the same time vegetables like onions and tomatoes have been getting scarce and expensive due to flood damage. But life goes on.

We've read in *Barricada*, the Sandinista newspaper, that 100 civilians were killed in *contra* attacks in August alone. What makes this really hit home, however, was a conversation I had recently with Carlos, a Nicaraguan engineer whom I'd met on retreat during Holy Week. Just back from the mountains of Jinotega, where he works on clean-water projects, he told me about seeing corpses with their eyes gouged out and burned bodies inside a blown-up car. The worst of it is knowing that as a government employee he's exactly the kind of person the *contras* like to target. A major part of their strategy is to keep the benefits of the revolution from spreading into the countryside. And yet teachers, health-care workers, agronomists and engineers continue to risk their lives by working in the war zone; this is what I think of when I read in the *New York Times* that the poor *contras* are starving for lack of humanitarian aid.

The opposition political leaders are still in jail for their part in organizing the riot/demonstration in Nandaime in July that I wrote about in the last newsletter. (They've got a six-month sentence, but it wouldn't surprise me if the government splashily pardoned them right before the next vote on *contra* aid.) It turns out that the judge at their trial, Ariel Jiménez, is the brother-in-law of a woman Peter works with. He is a dedicated young Sandinista, recently sent in to replace the old judge in Granada, who was a hold-over from the time of Somoza. He regularly gets death threats from the old guard in Granada who miss the comfortable corruption of the old days. Of course *La Prensa* hates him, and even the *New York Times* has mentioned his name unfavorably. To explain the funniest part of the Nandaime incident, however, I have to tell you about Aldo.

Aldo is the ex-mental patient who has been the terror of the UCA campus for the last couple years. He stalks up and down screaming and swearing at no one in particular. He brandishes a machete. He tries to talk to women. He dresses up in bizarre costumes—an Arab one day and a pirate the next. Last year he broke someone's arm. Recently he's taken to helping the landscaping crew. For some reason, the University administration has never managed to get him recommitted. In any case, he disappeared for several weeks in July, and everyone breathed a sigh of relief.

It turns out that he was one of the brave democratic activists who were arrested by the totalitarian Sandinistas at Nandaime. It's rumored that the US Embassy arranged transportation for people to go down there and that they even paid demonstrators to participate, but I doubt you'd have to pay Aldo very much to throw rocks and yell. In any case, the Sandinistas held Aldo for three weeks and then released him because they decided he wasn't responsible for his actions. At the UCA we were all amazed that it took them so long to figure that out—typical Sandinista inefficiency! At the same time, everyone groaned when he showed up on campus again—"He's the one they should have held onto."

One of our regrets as we get closer to our departure date is that we haven't gotten out of Managua more often. Peter went to Santo Tomás in Chontales to visit the Olympia Construction Brigade during Holy Week, while I went on a silent retreat at a Jesuit center outside of Granada. In May we went to Matagalpa for the weekend, and in July we visited Rosanne Fischer, a friend of a friend who works in León with the Minnesota sister-state project. We've been to the beach a couple times. But that's it. And it's too bad, because most of the best of Nicaragua is outside of Managua, which is a sprawling suburbs of a city, rebuilt without a downtown core after the 1972 earthquake, and now full of petty hustlers and war refugees.

León, in the flat, hot cotton country, and Matagalpa, in the cool, hilly coffee country, are gracious old colonial towns, where there's less noise, less diesel fumes and an old white plaster church with a bell tower on every block. León has an 18th century university campus off the central plaza—a far cry from the post-earthquake prefab of the UCA. It also has a lot of bullet-pocked and shell-shattered walls left over from the insurrection. The thing that moved me most, however, was visiting the ruins of the National Guard interrogation center— the Sandinistas blew the roof off, planted flowers, and turned it into a public park. But no one can forget that only a little over nine years ago, teen-age street fighters were being tortured in those cement cubicles. The statue in front shows one young man stooping to lift another. The message, Rosanne told us, is that you must never leave a wounded *compañero* behind.

So why don't we get out of the city more often? The answer is the bus system. To get on a bus leaving Managua, at least on weekends, you have to embroil yourself in a riot of pushing and shoving. People refuse to wait in line. They climb over the guard rails. They knock down old ladies. They trample on small children. After waiting for an hour and a half, the only reason we were able to get a ticket for León was that the seller closed the window and went to get the police, who forced people to stand in line. Miraculously, once we got tickets, we were even able to get seats, but I shared mine with a man, a woman and five children. And once we were thoroughly wedged in, the woman decided it was time to change the baby's diaper. Then the bus got a flat tire and we all had to get off and get back on again. Going to Matagalpa, we stood up for three hours, jammed in contorted positions and barely able to move. Despite these conditions, there are people who make their living as vendors by getting on these buses for short distances and fighting their way down the aisles selling pastries and fruit drinks. When some people got off and I finally got a seat, one of them rested her tub of pastries on my head for a while as she sold to the people around me. Even after that my problems were not over, because the woman sitting next to me was infested with some kind of ferocious insect which jumped happily onto me, leaving itching welts all down that side of my body for a week.

In other words, it's worth getting out of Managua occasionally, but I couldn't handle it every weekend (though some of my out-of-town students do). One of the great attractions of our trip to the Habitat for Humanity project in Puertas Viejas in late July (which Peter is writing about, along with some other big news) was that transportation was provided. Not only that, the Habitat people lent us their truck for the day so we could go to Esquipulas, thirty kilometers off the main road, to try and look up a friend of a friend, a priest from Connecticut who lives and works there. Although the priest was unfortunately out of town that day, our visit to Esquipulas was one of our best experiences in Nicaragua, and I'd like to tell you about it by quoting from the journal entry I wrote the next day:

The rutted dirt road to Esquipulas is really beautiful. Like much of rural Nicaragua, this is cattle country—some pasture, some forest. But the further in you go, the higher the mountains climb, jagged, remote and lushly green. Shacks of sticks and mud squat at the edge of dizzying hillsides, looking out onto hundreds of miles of peaks. Along the road we passed a whole lot of cows, families and communities of cows, mommy, daddy and baby cows, ambling along with their sharp horns, bony flanks and fat bellies, guided by small boys on skinny horses. We gave rides to any number of people—carrying milk cans, bundles of firewood, baskets of fruit, live chickens, machetes, small children. It's a long walk through there if no one stops.

Esquipulas is a typical Nicaraguan town, with dirt streets full of dogs, pigs and children, white plaster houses with red tile roofs, and a big old white church facing the grassy plaza. Lots of graffiti, most of it trying to promote the military service: "Volunteers for the Homeland! Join up!" We parked the truck in front of the rectory, and of course Padre Tomás was not there—he went to Managua yesterday. We left a note for him with the teenager in his office, sat and prayed in the church for a while, and then walked around town. We wanted to buy some bread and fruit, but no one was selling much of anything—the food shortage is not unique to Managua. We got lots of stares as we walked through the streets. Most people greeted us with *Adios* and a few tried out their English. We finally ended up having milk drinks in a little *comedor*. With all the cows, milk is the one thing in abundance.

I was making noises about wanting to take a walk—Esquipulas is set on the edge of a hill dropping down to a river valley with tall green mountains towering all around. Peter said his legs were tired from squatting on a roof all day yesterday, but he finally agreed to walk with me to the edge of town to see the view where the hill dropped off. And once we were there, he suddenly changed his mind and decided to keep going.

It was a sparkling clear day with the sun glaring off the white dirt road into our eyes, but the air was fresh and cool. We walked down a long gradual hill, past cornfields, banana trees, small houses, muddy waterfalls—and always above us the green mountains, woodland and pastureland, spiraling east into *contra* country, the *zona de guerra*. What a gift it is to walk along a quiet country road in the midst of so much beauty after months in the city—really a gift from God. Peter and I walked along slowly and didn't say very much, but I could feel my heart growing and unfolding in the sun, everything quiet except for the birds. Peace. Peace.

A mile or two down the road, we came to the bridge over the river, with a crossroads on the far side. Peter announced that he didn't feel like walking any further, but at least we walked over to the road sign so we could orient ourselves. North to San Ramon and Santa Rita. East to Muy Muy and Matiguas. There was a crowd of women waiting for a ride, and one *cachorro** in camouflage with his AK-47. They all laughed and asked us if we were planning to walk to Muy Muy. I wish! But we turned back and went to sit by the river. The water was clean but silty, running fast and shallow around large boulders. We sat down on a rock in the shade. A boy of about twelve was fishing among the boulders with a piece of string. He paid no attention to us. But the old *campesino* who was watching the water with his small grandson approached us and began to talk about fishing. Did Peter like to fish? There were some fish in this river, but for real fishing you had to go down the road three kilometers towards San Ramon, to the big river. That was the place to fish! He was going there tomorrow. Too bad the rains were piling up so much sand.

They drifted away, and we watched the kid fishing while a couple guys showed up on a motorcycle with a cake of soap and went under the bridge to bathe. I really wanted to go wading, but I was afraid it would attract too much attention. But I remembered that one rarely regrets going wading, so I took my shoes off and splashed around. The sand was soft underfoot, and the water was deliciously cool. I remembered I had a pair of jogging shorts in my day pack. A few moments later I was paddling along in the current, which was sweeping me slowly toward the boulders. There is nothing more refreshing than swimming in a little river, especially when you're not sure you ought to. I only stayed in for a little while, but I came out all tingling and happy.

A few minutes later the *cachorro* got tired of sitting in the

---

Cachorro, meaning "cub," is the popular nickname for young men doing their military service dust at the crossroads and decided to come down and talk to us. His name was Luís, he was from Estelí, he'd made it through eighteen months of the two year military service. The last five months he'd been stationed at the base in Esquipulas, which was a nice rest because there weren't any *contras* around. A year ago he was in combat over by Matiguas and got a grenade fragment in the back of his skull. It's still there and it still hurts. Five of his buddies died in that battle. A group of *contras* had come out of the woods with their hands up announcing they wanted to take part in the amnesty the Sandinistas were offering. But this was a trick, and they were followed by a lot more *contras* with guns who opened fire.

Before Luís was called up by the military, he was in his fifth year of high school and studying accounting at night. I asked him if he planned to return to his studies when he finished his service, and he said no, studying was worthless. He wants to go to Canada, where he has relatives, at least to visit. But he's not convinced he's going to survive that long. He's known people to be killed within seven days of the end of their service.

As we started up the hill again, we were overtaken by two boys, aged about twelve and nine. The bigger one was carrying a bag and a machete; the smaller one was carrying a bundle of firewood almost as big as he was. "Going to Esquipulas?" the older one asked. He was about to start up a trail, which he said was a short-cut. So we followed him. It was steep, climbing abruptly through green rocky fields with views of the valley and the mountains. The kid with the firewood suffered a lot more than we did. The sweat was standing out on his forehead and he said not a word the whole climb. But the other kid started talking to us. He told us he'd known the young Danish woman who was killed in Managua a few months ago—he'd picked coffee with her. He wanted to know if it was the *contras* who had killed her. We said no, it was robbers. He said the *contras* used to come through this area about once a month. There's a man on the other side of the hill that they visit. They've kidnapped a lot of people picking coffee. They kidnapped his sister but she escaped and is now in Costa Rica. He told us about finding a woman coffee picker that the *contras* had taken—her clothes ripped off as if the wind had blown them away and all the buttons gone. She was wrapped in the rags of her blouse and her skirt. But she was alive. And he talked about the new health center in Esquipulas, built two years ago. They'll sell you medicine when you have a cough much cheaper than the drug store. We came to a fork in the trail. "One way is to the health center and my house, the other way is to the church." We'd already told him we were here to visit Padre Tomás. "He's tall like I am," the kid had said. "He said the Mass for my sister's wedding." We thanked him for showing us the trails and said good-bye. His name was Marco.

Back at the church Padre Tomás had still not returned. We talked to the housekeeper and with her we looked at the little shrine for Oscar Romero by the door of the rectory. There was a photograph of his icon, with a quote saying that "they persecute us because we are on the side of the poor." There was a photo of him leading a procession. And there was a photo of him lying on the church floor in his vestments with blood all over his face and the nuns standing over him and sobbing. Then there was a long list of people from near-by towns who had been killed by the contras, with photos of many of them. The housekeeper pointed to one: "My cousin." There were tears in her eyes. "Monseñor Romero is with us in our suffering," said the message at the bottom of the shrine.

We drove back to Puertas Viejas on the long bumpy road, so we could connect with our ride back to Managua.

And so we came back to Managua, a little relieved to get out of the Puertas Viejas mud, and I'm now a month into the second semester at the UCA. I'm teaching English Composition I and III; unfortunately the lower-level class has forty students in it, so I spend a lot of time correcting papers. Nevertheless, I find that I really enjoy teaching writing, and hope to continue doing so when I get back to the States. I'm also working on a really exciting curriculum development project with two other teachers and a group of volunteer students. I'll write more about this in our next and last newsletter, which we'll probably send out around the end of October. The School of Translation is, by the way, looking for English teachers to start next March. The pay is lousy, but the students are great.

I want to make my ritual plea for LETTERS. When we don't get any mail for a while, we have no way of knowing if this is the fault of the postal system or if all of our friends have forgotten us. And you have no idea how much hearing from you means to us! So please make the attempt.

Lots of love,
Julia

Peter

The big news from this end and the reason I have time to write is that on August 28, I managed to fall off my bicycle and break my collarbone. I wish I could say it happened by hitting one of Managua's famous potholes or because of something dramatic like escaping a *contra* ambush, but I must admit it was due to my own foolishness. Julia and I were riding back from Mass at the University when I tried to ride close enough to pinch her, lost my balance and went flying onto the cobblestones. It seems my shoulder suffered most of the impact; the only other problem was a lot of skin scraped off my elbow. Fortunately I was wearing my helmet so a possible head injury was avoided. As a result of this I have been out of action for two weeks, and it will be at least two more weeks before I can return to work. I was at the doctor again yesterday—he said my collarbone appeared to be mending fine. I thank God, pray for patience and try to be mindful of the Nicaraguans who are really suffering. A little consolation is that the break is on the left side so I can still write and help with domestic chores. Julia says my fit of adolescent behavior causing the injury was a good sign because it means I'm not growing old prematurely. She has been wonderful in the role of nursemaid even though it means extra work on top of an already busy schedule at the University.

The last week in July was our only chance to get out of town together for more than a weekend, so we took advantage of the opportunity. We were able to visit and work on a Habitat for Humanity project in Puertas Viejas, about eighty miles north of

Managua. This was far enough out of Managua to experience the Nicaraguan countryside yet still safely south of the war zone.

Habitat for Humanity is an international organization, based in Georgia, working to build sturdy, affordable housing for poor people world-wide. Habitat provides the start-up money, equipment and technical assistance, while the future home-owners supply the labor. They are involved in all aspects of the project from design and site layout to the actual construction of the houses. The partners, as they are called, are expected to work a certain number of hours on the project and in return receive a house with an affordable interest-free mortgage. All money paid on these mortgages is used to fund new projects.

Millard Fuller, the founder of Habitat, writes in his latest book, *No More Shacks*, "We might disagree on how to preach or how to dress or how to baptize or how to take communion or even what communion is for. But we can all pick up a hammer and, sharing the love of Christ, we can begin to drive nails. Thank God we can agree on a nail!" An example of this was when Jimmy Carter, a Habitat supporter, and Daniel Ortega went to the dedication of the first Habitat project in Nicaragua. They laid up some cement block together, spoke about how it was an example of the love of Christ and Christian action, and handed out Bibles to some of the new Habitat homeowners.

Habitat currently has ten projects going in Nicaragua. The one in Puertas Viejas, a town of about two hundred people, includes twenty new houses. In keeping with the Habitat philosophy of using local materials, the houses are being constructed of rammed earth blocks, made on site, with the wood for doors, window shutters and roof rafters milled on site from Nicaraguan logs. The only thing imported is the donated zinc roofing, and they are experimenting with a locally made roof tile as an alternative to that. These are very simple three-room houses with cement floors, but they are a big improvement over the vermin-infested shacks the people are living in now.

We spent the week working alongside some of the people who will live in the houses when finished. One who really impressed us was Doña Julia, a woman in her mid-forties who recently had moved back to Puertas Viejas after working as a maid in Managua for a number of years. She had never had any construction experience but learned fast and is now one of the most skilled people on the project. Whatever the activity, she was in the middle of it, whether laying block, tying rebar together for connecting beams, or organizing the other workers to help keep things running smoothly. Although already a grandmother, she still has a young daughter to look after, and when her new house is ready, they will be able to move out of the crowded two-room house they have been sharing with eight other family members.

Not all of the people working on the project are Sandinista supporters, but they are all living examples of the revolutionary spirit. By working together they are empowering themselves and creating better conditions for the community that would never exist without this kind of cooperation. For sure there are problems with in-fighting and people stealing from the project supplies, but these are small in comparison to the new houses going up and the improved quality of life they represent. Some graffiti I recently saw etched in the cement of the sidewalk read "*¿Quien Vive? Cristo Vive o Sandino Vive?*" The question being "Who Lives? Christ or Sandino?" I don't see why the spirit of both can't be co-motivators in the struggle for an improved society here in Nicaragua.

One thing that made us think about this lately was the big open-air Mass we went to on the Feast of the Assumption, celebrated in the main plaza by Cardinal Obando himself. He was flanked by his auxiliary bishops, most of the parish priests, groups of young seminarians, and about one hundred nuns in full habit. When we arrived, the tail-end of a long procession was making its way into the plaza. This included parade-type floats with statues of Mary and little girls dressed up like angels, uniformed marching bands in perfect step, and thousands of people carrying banners and palm branches. The drum majors amused Julia; she pointed out that you never see Sandinista troops marching in step like that.

The backdrop for all this was the earthquake-damaged shell of the old Cathedral. A number of people had climbed out onto the ledge a good thirty feet above the steps where the altar was set up. The Managua weather, not wanting to let us down, cooked up a steamer. It must have been at least one hundred degrees with the usual high humidity. All the umbrellas used as sun-shades made it hard to see, and the vendors added to the confusion by constantly winding through the crowd selling soft drinks and food items.

After much bell-ringing and many cheers of "¡*Viva el Papa!*" and "¡*Viva Nicaragua Catolica!*" the Mass proceeded. I didn't expect much, as Obando's theology is as conservative as his politics. I was actually surprised that a lay-woman did one of the readings. In his homily Obando tried to equate the life of Mary to that of Esther in the Old Testament. Both being chosen, one by a king and one by God, they were thus saved from a death that was certain to befall those around them. This was followed by long prayers for the suffering people of Nicaragua. I would like to think Obando is sincere in these prayers, but I know the previous Wednesday he refused, as he does every week, to meet with a group of mothers of those kidnapped or killed by the *contras*. They gather for a weekly vigil outside his office and at best he sends out a priest to pray with them.

After Mass we were standing on the steps of the National Palace looking over the scene when a middle-aged Nicaraguan woman came up and roughly asked if we were Catholics. When we said yes, she wanted to know if we liked the Mass. We told her it was nice and interesting, and she went away seemingly satisfied. A few minutes later she was back with a friend to ask where we were from. When we told her the United States, she said that too many internationalists who come to Nicaragua are communists. "I want you to go back to the US and tell people we're not communists, we're good Catholics." In my poor Spanish I tried to explain that many people in the US realize that Nicaraguans are not communists. She said "You go back there and tell people that we're suffering." At this she left, shouting "¡*Viva Nicaragua Catolica!*" with the rest. We went our way before getting into a fight over theology or politics.

That evening we went to another Mass at the Maria de Los Angeles Church. This one is well-known for its liberation theology and rousing music. The regular priest and the band were not there, so it was much lower key than my first experience of it, which had impressed me as being mostly a performance for the international visitors in the congregation. Here an older Portuguese priest said Mass and spoke about how Mary continues to suffer with the mothers in Nicaragua who have lost loved ones in the war—very different than Obando's portrayal of her as a privileged Queen. Some of the women who had lost family members were present and helped lead the prayers. I felt more comfortable in this setting and appreciated this image of Mary a lot more—although some of the internationalists seemed disappointed not to be getting the whole show.

The work on the Hans Gutiérrez project continues to progress slowly. In August we had a construction brigade from Marin County, California helping us for two weeks. The tools and money they brought gave us the means and incentive to start construction again. I was enjoying working out there every day and was looking forward to a four to six week stretch of it when my accident took me out of action. Misael, my Nicaraguan lead man, is back on the job and supervising the work in my absence.

The teachers have started taking the main group of students out to the land three or four days a week. They spend part of the morning in the classroom and then some time outside doing brush clearing and garden work. After this they eat their lunches and head back to town. This is great for Walter, who continues to work like a regular on the construction crew. It means he gets to spend time with his buddies and has on-going contact with cooperative staff people while I'm not there.

Our year in Nicaragua is beginning to wind down, and we're already making travel plans to leave in early December. We hope to see many of you on the West Coast around Christmastime. Until then, our P.O. Box is always accepting letters...

In peace,
Peter

MANAGUA, NICARAGUA
November 6, 1988

By the time you get this, we may have already left Nicaragua.
We're flying to Mexico City a month from today on December
6, and riding buses north from there. We're still planning to
spend time in San Diego, the Bay Area and Portland, arriving in
Seattle (down and out) shortly before Christmas. I won't say I'm
not looking forward to leaving. This year has been a real gift in
so many ways, and I wouldn't have missed it, and I've even spent
some beautiful days at the beach recently, but in general it's been
really hard. I find that daily life here leaves me tired most of the
time, and I think the whole country is tired. The Sandinistas
who hold onto the vision of the revolution are living on black
coffee and neglecting their families to keep Nicaragua limping
forward into the future. A few of them have been at it for twenty
years or more, and most of them for at least ten. Can they keep
it up forever? Perhaps. They're a lot tougher than I am.

The upcoming election of George Bush, of course, means
that US pressure will continue and life will go on being difficult
here for some time. Reagan administration policies in general
and the *contra* war in particular are the one single factor that has
made the Sandinista ideals of a better life for the Nicaraguan
people (health care, education, economic self-sufficiency...)
most difficult to achieve. Meanwhile, the money the CIA
throws around to foment fear and suspicion between the government and the opposition has made political pluralism and the
mixed economy rather shaky as well. I don't think that the US
will succeed in over-throwing the revolution as both the *contras*
and the internal opposition are weak; money and media attention are no substitute for a political platform and a popular

following. However, it's hard for the revolution to accomplish much in the climate of apathy, discontent and anxiety that the present conditions create. And one thing more I'd like to say about the war is that Socorrito, the maid in our house, had eight cousins drafted in May, and by now three are dead and one has a serious leg wound.

Then on Saturday October 22, into the middle of all this came Hurricane Joan (or *"Juana la Huracana"* as she's "affectionately" known here, after the popular *salsa* tune, *"Juana la Cubana"*). The Sandinistas had word she was on her way several days ahead of time, and set about taking precautions. They declared a National Emergency, cleaned up the storm sewers around Managua, piled sand bags around public buildings, evacuated people from low-lying areas and the entire Atlantic Coast, sent the Red Cross around to collect blood....Meanwhile the opposition newspaper *La Prensa* was saying that the government was over-reacting, they were just trying to militarize the whole country. And for once I almost agreed with them. I'm not sure exactly why I was so certain that the hurricane would fizzle out, but in any case I was wrong and Chicken Little was right. Even on Sunday, the day after the storm, when we rode our bikes around Managua and saw trees down but no roofs blown off, we thought that all the frenzied preparations had been just the result of the general anxiety that Nicaragua is suffering, which leads people to always expect the worst.

Then on Monday we saw the pictures of Bluefields and Corn Island in the newspaper. On the Atlantic Coast the winds were close to 200 miles an hour, and they smashed all the little houses and fishing boats into kindling sticks. Ninety-five percent of the buildings were left uninhabitable. The bells in the cathedral at Bluefields were ringing wildly in the storm till the steeple toppled over. The headlines in the newspaper read "Here Stood Bluefields." And I began to realize that the inconveniences of having classes cancelled and two days of intermittent power and water were very minor inconveniences indeed. Even in Managua, which missed the worst of the storm, there were eighty houses lost when the Tipitapa River flooded. A friend of mine at work told me that her Sandinista husband was out running around that neighborhood Saturday night in the wind and the rain trying to get people to evacuate, but many refused to leave their houses till they saw the waters rising. Two student volunteers on the same mission were trapped by the flood waters for a while, but luckily escaped. "And Marcos can't even swim!" my friend added.

By Wednesday afternoon at the UCA they finally got around to organizing brigades to help the refugees, and I volunteered. One gets tired of sitting around selfishly and doing nothing in the face of national tragedy. We were to help at a refugee center for people evacuated from the Atlantic Coast—1500 of them in a hastily converted high school. As it turned out, the brigades weren't very well organized, and we spent most of Thursday sitting around waiting for something to happen. Then, out of some misplaced sense of martyrdom, the group decided to work all night, which I refused to do. Still, I spent the better part of Thursday afternoon unloading truckloads of milk, rice and mattresses, and then showed up bright and early Friday morning to help dig drainage ditches. By then, of course, the rest of the brigade was exhausted.

Things were mildly disorganized at the refugee center, but I was nonetheless impressed at how well things were going there. People seemed to be getting fed on schedule, the refugees had been organized to help with the cleaning, a clinic had been set up, and public health announcements came over the loud-speakers every few minutes. Friday morning a theater group came and put on a show with fantastic costumes in the central courtyard; after that, there was music and drawing for the children (lovely pictures of islands, villages, palm trees and fishing boats), and Padre Ricardo from the UCA said Mass in the auditorium. A catechist from Bluefields gave the homily: he said that as they went back to rebuild their towns, this was an opportunity to rebuild their hearts at the same time. I was moved—these were people who had lost everything, and I would have expected more overt despair. But they seemed to be coping. I was particularly impressed by the kids running around in little gangs and somehow managing to stay amused. When we were unloading trucks on Thursday, they all insisted on helping, even the little ones. That was where the action was, and they wanted to be part of it.

Late morning on Friday, just as the UCA brigade was sputtering out from lack of sleep, my friend Susan showed up with a box of books from the children's library, and we both read aloud to a wildly enthusiastic audience for three hours until we were completely hoarse. The only regret I heard was from one little boy who missed his baseball bat: "In Bluefields the kids play baseball all the time," he said wistfully.

And of course reconstruction is going to be a very tough job. The resources simply don't exist in this country to carry it out. Not only houses were destroyed—crops were lost, bridges were washed away, tropical rain forest was mowed down, the fishing industry will take years to recover. Seven years ago, the Sandinistas planted a lot of African palm oil trees in the vicinity of Bluefields. They would have started producing this year, but now they're all gone. The economists are saying that this storm caused more economic damage than even the 1972 earthquake that destroyed most of Managua. The one lucky thing is that only perhaps 200 lives were lost in the whole country—most of them to flooding in remote areas where the Sandinistas couldn't get in to warn people in time. But all in all, it's been a horrible disaster, and Nicaragua is going to need lots of help from the rest of the world just to get through the next year. And yet from what we hear, the US isn't planning to contribute a penny, even through the Red Cross. (Up to now, the Cubans have responded far more than anyone else.) As for the *contras*, their response so far has been to attack a relief truck heading for the flooded town of El Rama and kill three or four of the occupants. Classes were cancelled for a week at the UCA, which means that finals have been postponed for a week. Consequently, my last few days in Managua I'll be packing with one hand and marking exams with the other. But, as I said, that kind of thing is a minor inconvenience compared with what the whole country is suffering. The students have found it difficult to come back to business letters and paragraph structure after all the worry and excitement—but, as I tell them, Nicaragua in 1988 is one crisis after another, and yet I have to keep teaching and they have to keep studying (although sometimes it feels like fiddling while Rome burns).

Along with teaching English Composition this semester,

I've been working with another teacher on a curriculum development project that I'd like to tell you about. My colleague hopes to use the results of it to develop a new textbook for the School of Translation which will be more relevant to the situation here than our current British model. ("Fred and Liz win the lottery! Should she buy a fur coat? Or a Mercedes? Or both?!?") We're working with the ideas of the Brazilian educator Paulo Freire. He's done most of his work with literacy, but his central ideas can easily be applied to language teaching. His contention is that education should involve "praxis," the union of reflection and action. By reflecting critically together on their own situations, students can come to a new understanding of them and prepare to take action together to improve things. Since an essential part of this process is dialogue, or in other words communication, and as "communication" is the goal of the modern language teacher, consciousness-raising and better English work very nicely together. And we're also trying to incorporate some cross-cultural content into this which will be more enlightening than the canned view of British or US society presented in most text books (for example, we want to use Bruce Springsteen's songs of economic dislocation).

One of Freire's ideas is that the students themselves should help to define course content. To this end, we worked intensively with a seminar group of volunteer students. Through brainstorming, prioritizing and reflecting on their own lives, they helped us come up with a list of topics of concern to Nicaraguan university students (from alcoholism to water pollution to the psychological effects of the war), and then they worked with us to find concrete ways of illustrating these topics so that they can be analyzed effectively according to Freirian methodology. We were able to spend a week trying out our materials in an intermediate English class, and they went over very well. In order to focus on the question of "who does the housework?" we gave them a selection from the English translation of a poem by the Sandinista feminist poet, Gioconda Belli. The following is one verse from it:

> ....Over there one is dragging her sandals
> looking at her damp fingers
> she's coming from the factory

with a handkerchief tied around her head
the machines still echo in her ears
In the place she dreams
there are children crowding noisily
around the chairs and the tables
a big bundle of clothes to wash
the raw vegetables
the pots familiar with no other hands
but hers... *

After discussing this thoroughly according to Freirean methodology, we had the students write and act out skits based on looking for solutions to the unfair division of household chores. This is a hot topic among Nicaraguan women right now, with the men still kicking and screaming. The skits turned out to be terrific—well-written, well-acted, and offering lots of food for further discussion afterwards. The central insight that came out of them was the need for a strong sense of personal conviction as one tries to make changes in society or in one's own life.

All of this has been tremendously exciting to me, because if I have one goal as an ESL (English as a Second Language) teacher, it's student self-expression. I mean, I'll work to help them learn their grammar, but that's not what makes my job exciting. I hope a new text book comes out of our work (so far our project has been disrupted by midterms, an international youth conference, a student rebellion and a hurricane), but in any case I'm looking forward to using and developing this methodology more when I go back to the States. We presented our project at the UCA Forum for Scientific Development and it was well-received. (Talk about fiddling while Rome burned— the forum was three days after the hurricane! I know I'll always remember my first professional presentation, in Spanish and to an almost empty hall...) My colleagues have been asked to bring it to the National Forum, which will be held at the University in León in March. Hopefully we'll get a larger audience there;

---

*Gioconda Belli, translated by Steven F. White, in "Women, Poetry, New Nicaraguan Culture," *Envio*, Vol. 7, No. 83, Managua, Nicaragua, 1988.

the principles of Paulo Freire are also the principles of Nicaraguan education enunciated after the Revolution, but so far they haven't been applied to language teaching here, or much in higher education at all. There's still a lot of rote-learning going on, with no opportunity for critical reflection.

I must say I look forward to seeing all of you. I don't know what kind of fund-raising relief efforts for Nicaragua are going on in your environs, but I really encourage you to contribute to them. If nothing else, try the International Red Cross. They do good work here. Take care of yourselves, and think about sharing a bottle of red wine with us when we see you next.

Love,
Julia

Peter

November 16, 1988

I just arrived back in Managua Monday evening the 14th after spending two weeks on the road with the Walk for Peace and Life. This is a peace walk between Managua and the town of Las Manos on the border with Honduras. I left the group in Estelí to come back for a visit with Julia and to work on this newsletter. If all goes well, I will return to the walk on Sunday the 20th and continue on to the border, arriving on November 30.

Before I go on, I suppose I should say a little about the Hans Gutiérrez project for those of you who are interested. Construction at the site has been moving slowly and will soon stop due to lack of funds. The workers are almost done with a system of steel-reinforced cement pedestals and connecting ground beams. This will support the steel box columns for the roof structure that will span the walls we put up earlier in the year.

I had some good times working out there but was often frustrated with the slow progress due to limited resources, bad design decisions and unfavorable weather conditions. The most positive thing for me was my work with Walter. He has become a good buddy during the year, learned some construction skills and developed an improved sense of self-worth. I have also enjoyed my regular visits with his family in Ciudad Sandino. His mother makes great tortillas and always gives me more than I pay for.

As for the rest of the students, I haven't had much contact with them. They were going to the land for a while, but it was such a problem getting in there that the decision was made to hold classes at Frances Romero's house in Managua. Now they are on vacation till after New Year, and the teachers are taking a course in neuro-psychology being offered by some people from Seattle.

I still think the project is a good one and very necessary for Nicaragua. There is talk of getting a new piece of land that is more accessible; I feel this would be a positive step. The project also needs a big donation, which may be coming from the Norwegian government, as well as new people with skills in special education and construction. I wish them well, and hope the dream becomes a reality.

In any case, so far my experience on the Walk has been wonderful, and it's done a lot to improve my attitude towards life here. As Julia already told you, the day-to-day struggle to survive has taken its toll on us. By the end of October, I was disgusted with life in Managua, frustrated with my work situation and really needing to get out of the city for a while. The opportunity to go walking came at the perfect time, and I decided it was a chance not to be missed.

This walk was the idea of Hediki Sasamori, a Japanese Buddhist monk who lives in Nicaragua. He is here to support and draw attention to the Nicaraguans' struggle for peace. His most recent action before this walk was a forty day fast and vigil in the Plaza of the Revolution. He began this fast on August 6, the anniversary of the bombing of Hiroshima. It was during these forty days that he came up with the idea of walking from Managua north into the war zone near Honduras.

We left Managua the morning of November 1 with about 150 people. Most of them were only with us for the day, but the numbers made for high spirits and good visibility. Along for the morning part of the walk were Fr. Miguel D'Escoto, Maryknoll priest and Foreign Minister of Nicaragua, who led a previous peace walk through northern Nicaragua in 1986, and Brian Wilson, the US veteran whose legs were cut off by a train as he attempted to block a shipment of weapons to the *contras*. Now a Nicaraguan folk hero, he managed the morning walk just fine with his prosthesis. There were also many Nicaraguans from the evangelical churches and Catholic base communities, a sprinkling of internationalists from North America and Europe, and Sasamori beating his hand drum and chanting. The twenty-three kilometers out to Tipitapa that first day made it the longest of our walk. We arrived in the park late that afternoon and were greeted by music and words of welcome from the mayor as dusk closed in.

On the road the next morning between Tipitapa and San Benito we had one of the special moments that have made this walk such a strong experience. We stopped at the home of one of the local Mothers of Heroes and Martyrs. She had lost two sons in the fighting, and the picture of one of them was propped up on the front porch surrounded by flowers. It was All Souls Day, so it was very fitting that we be there to help honor her dead sons. Sasamori has a special prayer he offers to the spirit of these dead heroes which is very powerful. Burning incense, he chants and beats his hand drum loudly. He then asks the mothers, and anyone else who chooses, to offer some incense and call out the name of their dead son, relative or friend. In most of the towns we walk through, our first stop is at the cemetery to honor the *caídos*, those who have fallen in the fighting. Every time, I am deeply moved by this. There is usually a group of the Mothers present and other people from town who have come to walk with us and help honor the dead heroes. The Mothers of the Heroes and Martyrs are some of the most inspiring people I have met in Nicaragua. They have suffered and lost so much and yet they are able to keep struggling and inspire others to do the same. I think we in the US can learn a lot from these women who have embraced the pain and loss and are able to move forward with strength.

In La Trinidad we met a woman who has lost her husband, her brother and seven nephews in the fighting. She has another grown son living with her who is suffering severe mental problems due to his experience in the war. This would leave most people depressed and bitter, yet she is one of the most warm, loving people we have encountered. It's people like this who keep Nicaragua moving forward against the US-backed aggression. They are very clear about what it is their loved ones died for and what they continue to work towards. They are also very clear on the difference between the policies of the US government and the people of the US who support them in their struggle for peace with dignity.

Almost every day people from the town we are leaving walk with us and usually some from the next town come out to join us. This includes large numbers of school children, who swell our ranks and spirits with their bright eyes and high energy. Nicaragua is full of children, and their future is dependent on the truggle for peace and the fulfilment of the revolution.

Sasamori has been making paper peace cranes everywhere we go. This has been a big hit with the children. Of course they all want one, so the other walkers help out and we show the older children and teachers in every town how to make them. Sasamori recounts the tradition that if you concentrate on a prayer while making a thousand cranes, your prayer will be realized. He tells the story of Sadako, the little girl dying of leukemia after the bombing of Hiroshima, who succeeded in folding 990 of them.

And so we walk on through these little towns like El Madroño, Puertas Viejas, Las Calabazas, Chagüitillo and Santa Cruz, as well as bigger places like Darío, Sébaco and Estelí. The reception and attitude varies from one place to the next, but we have had a good exchange with the people everywhere we have stopped.

Of course some towns are more organized than others. In El Madroño we met some wonderful people, but the revolution hasn't changed their lives much. The woman I stayed with was born and raised there and seemed content with life as it was. She sounded a little sad that all her children and grandchildren move to other places in search of work, but she understands there is nothing for them to do in El Madroño. The power lines run along the highway only a few meters from their houses, yet there is no electricity in town and no community effort being made to get the necessary transformer to bring the power in. Also the water supply is not very good and runs low during the dry season, but nothing is being done about digging a community well. Although the revolution encourages people to organize and take action on these issues, in El Madroño the feeling is that they are waiting for things to be presented to them.

In contrast to this was the village of Chagüitillo, where the people are very organized and go after what they want. I couldn't believe all the progress they had made in four or five years. They have a community council that determines the needs, comes up with solutions, and then formulates and implements plans to make the changes a reality. This is what the revolution is all about, people working together to improve their collective conditions. In Chagüitillo this has led to the construction of an impressive child development center, an addition to the primary school and the start of construction on the secondary school so that the high school students won't have to commute to Sébaco to study. They also have a well-functioning farming cooperative on the edge of town and smaller coops for sewing and other light production to create jobs in the community. Certainly Chagüitillo has gotten a lot of international aid, but under the current conditions it is necessary, and the fact that they were ready for it and actively pursued it helped a lot.

Towns also differ in terms of which religious community comes out to walk with us. It is supposed to be an ecumenical peace walk, and for sure Sasamori is one of the most ecumenical people I know, and yet we still see conflict and division between the Catholics and Evangelicals. In most towns it has been the Evangelicals who have walked with us and shared in the evening gatherings. The priests tend to be conservative, and have told their parishioners not to participate in the walk. Other places the local Catholic base community has organized things for us, and this makes the Evangelicals stay away because they don't want to associate with the Catholics.

The only local priest who has come out to welcome us was Fr. Ernesto Bravo in La Trinidad. I heard one woman in town refer to him affectionately as *"Comandante Bravo."* He is very revolutionary and working hard to improve conditions for the people in town. The gathering that evening in front of his church was great. We had a few songs, a reading from scripture, testimony from Sasamori and Pastora (another walker), and a group discussion. I felt like better communication took place there than in the Evangelical gatherings where there is a lot of singing, loud preaching and no time for reflection and discussion. The next morning at Mass I witnessed a rare if not unheard of event. Fr. Bravo offered communion to everyone who came forward including Sasamori—there can't be many times when a Catholic priest has given communion to a Buddhist monk.

The best part of this walk for me has been the interaction with the people we meet along the road, in the homes we stay in, in the parks and community centers and wherever else we might be. To be able to talk, share ideas, worship and even cry with them has been an incredibly bonding experience. Also the chance to walk along the road past fields, rivers and villages, breathing the clean air and enjoying the beauty of the hills is allowing me to get a feeling for and a lasting image of the other Nicaragua that exists outside of Managua.

The other interesting thing I was involved in lately was helping out at the wheelchair repair shop at the Aldo Chavarría Rehabilitation Hospital. By late September my collar bone was healed enough to where I could do some light work. The hospital has had an old shop with a full-time mechanic; the idea of the new shop is to expand the facility and start training disabled Nicaraguans in wheelchair repair. They already have three apprentices with plans to bring on three more in January. These are all people in wheelchairs with permanent disabilities to their legs. The new shop isn't quite ready and is not officially open to take in repair work so I mostly hung out with the apprentices and helped them do what they could to organize tools and get work stations set up. Once the shop is open and word gets out I think they will have plenty of business. The low intensity war the US is waging against Nicaragua is causing a lot of physical and mental disabilities.

This expanded shop will help pick up some of the load by keeping existing chairs in working order and hopefully starting to build custom chairs on site. Conventional wheelchairs are almost useless except on flat smooth surfaces. People trying to get around town on their own need a lower-slung chair with good quality wheels, bearings and bicycle tires. There is already one place in Managua which builds custom chairs, but they are expensive and in short supply.

The disabled guys working at the shop have to travel long distances across town to and from work often in the rain and always in traffic that has little or no concern for their safety. There are no shoulders to the streets and the actual road surface is broken up with pot holes. Many of the streets are cobblestone — the vibration from these must be awful in a wheelchair. The public buses are always over-crowded and have no wheelchair access even if there was room.

I should mention that one objective of the *contra* war is to maim people rather than kill them, thus creating a greater strain on the system. It seems clear that the small land mines they use were designed for just this purpose. The rehabilitation hospitals are doing their best to handle the increased case loads. They are fitting people with prosthesis as they are available, giving them physical therapy and vocational training and setting them up with crutches and wheelchairs as needed. It's inspiring to see these efforts being carried out successfully in a society with such limited resources.

I just wish that Ronald Reagan, George Bush and the other policy makers could have some of these experiences. If they could only look into the eyes of the children, spend time with some of the mothers at the graves of their sons, and visit the rehabilitation hospitals or centers for those disabled by the war, they might find it hard to continue their support for the terrorist activity of the *contras* and what that is doing to this poor country.

Sasamori says we must struggle to transform the enemy within before we can have any hope of affecting the evil that is causing so much pain, suffering and unrest around us in the world. Let us all pray for the courage and strength to embrace that struggle.

Love,
Peter

After finishing the last letter home with Julia, Peter rejoined the peace walk from Managua to Los Manos on the Honduran border. These excerpts from his journal were written during and immediately following the walk. Although they are "letters to himself," they clarify and enrich the letters that Peter and Julia sent home during their time in Nicaragua.

Tuesday, November 22, Palacaguina

Left Managua Sunday morning after waiting for the rain to let up (but still) early, in order to beat the crowds....At the Roberto Huembes market, I found the line of people waiting for the bus to Estelí, and within twenty minutes I was on a bus heading north. There were seats to spare when we pulled out....In Estelí I only had to wait about thirty minutes for the bus to Somoto. After asking a number of people on the bus where I needed to get off for Pueblo Nuevo (where the walk was staying), I got off at the crossroads north of Condega....

The road west was for Pueblo Nuevo. By this time the sky was clearing, the sun had come out and my bus connections had been so good that I felt like God was making special efforts to guide my way. Waiting at the crossroads was a truck taking passengers for Pueblo Nuevo. I offered to pay the same fare as everyone else, but they wouldn't take it and gave me a seat up front with the driver and his helper. This was a beautiful ride over a dirt road through the hills. The noise of the engine made it hard for me to understand their Spanish, so the conversation was pretty choppy. When I asked how the war had gone in this area, the guy on my right said "we kicked the bastards out of here," explaining that "Nicaragua is a small country, but it has balls," and that "if the Yankees come, they will have problems with us."

I arrived at the park in Pueblo Nuevo soon after the walkers. The timing was perfect, as they were just assigning us to our houses for the night. I went with Greg and Francisco to a *hospedaje* (guest house) operated by Doña Cristina. This meant we had beds with sheets, great food and good company....Francisco was entertaining the family with origami peace cranes and flirting with Maria, the sixteen year old daughter....

Thursday, November 24, Somoto

...The people from Palacagüina met us at the crossroads on the highway and walked the three kilometers into town with us. As usual the first stop was in the cemetery....Again we had a group of the Mothers with us, some of them cried as Sasamori prayed and the smoke rose from the incense offerings. Others prayed while Sasamori softly banged his drum. These prayers come from a place of incredible pain, but also from strength....

I had a good family to stay with in Palacagüina. They had moved there after the first uprising in Estelí in 1978....In the evening I had dinner with Samuel, the man of the house....Samuel works at the meat-packing plant in Condega, which is a state-operated enterprise to process meat for export. He is a refrigeration and electronics technician who got his training in a correspondence course before the Triumph (of the revolution)....We talked about the economy, the required military service, the US government, and he talked a little about how bad the *contra* activity had been in '82 and '83....

Friday, November 25, Esperanza

Yesterday was Thanksgiving in the States. As I sit here thinking about everything I have to be thankful for, I am overwhelmed....The Nicaraguans who so freely accept us, walk with us and take us into their homes have helped me get a little more in touch with the unlimited love and mercy of God. I feel very small in comparison, in my own ability to love and forgive....

(At the cemetery in Yalagüina) I found myself getting disturbed by the children crowding around in their curiosity to see Sasamori and what he was doing. I realized that this is my own hang-up....so I closed my eyes and let the drum beat and the chanting carry me....As Sasamori finished and the group broke up....I stayed to pray in silence for a few minutes (for the young men who had died). I prayed that God might hold (them) and grant them the peace they probably never had in this life. I'm sure many went to their deaths without a clear sense of what they were fighting for. I have talked to some who are politically aware and committed to the revolutionary process yet are afraid of the armed conflict, so I can imagine how it is for those who haven't developed their values and ideas....

Wednesday, November 30, Dipilto

(In Totogalpa) I....was assigned to stay with Francisco and Sasamori. Our arrangements were fine except for the drunks who held down the tables in the bar at the back of the courtyard....Doña Isabel, whose house it was, didn't approve of the drinking, although it didn't disturb her enough to keep her from selling it to them for a profit. I had some good conversation with her, her daughter...and one of her grand-daughters. They all share two large houses along with other assorted family members....

The evening gathering in Totogalpa was interesting in that the Evangelicals and the Catholics both showed up, (although they) stood in separate groups. George and I were sitting across the street watching this, curious to see what would happen. Well, the Evangelicals, with Raúl in the lead, held forth for a while and then extended an invitation to the Catholics to come forward. You can tell by listening to the singing whether a group is Evangelical or Catholic. So we had some songs from the Catholics, who seemed a little timid, and then they moved back across the street. I'm glad that at least they came out instead of staying home like in so many of the other towns. So often we hear that the priest has told them....to avoid contact with us because....some of us are "communists"....

The last evening in Totogalpa, I was sitting outside writing. Once again I was interrupted, but it was all right, because it turned into a conversation with a guy who had recently completed his military service. He is working part time as a teacher's aide in the local school and trying to finish his own high school studies. He was pretty discouraged by the lack of jobs for returning *cachorros* and the government's inability to make good on the services promised them. It did seem like he was trying to do something about his own situation, although the rum he had been drinking won't help....

(In Ocotal) I was fortunate enough to be placed in the Casa Materna, with Raúl, Francisco, Calixto and Alicia....

The Casa Materna is one of the projects often referred to as "the fruit of the revolution," (although) at this point it is dependent on international aid, mostly from Sweden....It is a center for poor women from Ocotal and surrounding areas to come and prepare for giving birth....At the Casa Materna, they are provided with balanced meals, prenatal check-ups, exercise classes and a comfortable, clean place to stay in the weeks leading up to the birth. In return they do the cooking, cleaning and other daily chores to maintain the center. There is a sewing and crafts room where they make things for the gift shop....There is a staff of four or five women from Ocotal who...are working on a grant from the Swedish government for salary money. There is also a Maryknoll volunteer on the staff who is a nurse-midwife. It's the first project of its kind in the country, and hopes to be a model for similar centers in other cities. They have been open for a year, have already handled more than two hundred women and only lost two babies....

(On our tour the next morning we visited) the Hogar de Ancianos (Senior Citizens Home)....It turned out to be another wonderful project that has come to be since the revolution. It was specifically for people sixty years old or older who had no family to live with or ability to live on their own....We met them in a covered patio out in the garden area. They had prepared a little program of music, poetry and dancing. We then got a tour of the grounds where all the trees, flowers and vegetables were planted and cultivated by the residents....One woman who met us in the covered walkway was quite spunky and had a poem to recite. She tossed her cane aside saying she didn't need it, and proceeded to entertain us for the next ten minutes. When she was done we were introduced to a very elderly man who had known and fought with Sandino. He was supposed to recite verse as well, but was feeling dizzy and wasn't up to it. He did accept a kiss from Ligia and seemed to enjoy the attention of a young woman.

Marta, our guide for the morning, encouraged us to move on, so we headed out to a day center for children who are either war orphans or from large families who don't have the resources to take care of them....While we were there, they...put on an interesting and well-done skit depicting an attack by the Guardia Nacional in 1974. This was done silently, in costume with only music as a back drop. The boys playing the guard members had fierce-looking masks and wooden mock-ups of machine guns. They kept coming round and harassing a group of village women, raping them and beating one woman who was pregnant and lost the baby as a result. This was portrayed by a small plastic baby doll left lying on the floor after the attack. On the last visit the guard members shoot all the women and leave laughing.

None of the children performing the skit would have been alive in 1974, so it's interesting to see the story being maintained this way in the local folklore. It's good that the children are getting a sense of what Nicaragua was like before the revolution....

The walk to Dipilto was almost all uphill but beautiful through pine-covered hills. The air got cooler as we climbed....The road followed the river...(and) a couple times it crossed the river on bridges, so we got a good view of the river cascading over rocks as it fell towards the valley below. At other times I would leave the road and run to the edge of the cliff looking down into the river. This made some of the Nicas nervous, for fear of land mines. I told them I didn't believe God wanted to take me that way. I wasn't willing to feed into Raúl's paranoia....

Thursday, December 1, Las Manos

We walked up to the (Honduran) border at Las Manos yesterday morning with much joy, high spirits and many people who had come to walk with us for the last day. This morning we are sitting in the international zone between Nicaragua and Honduras. Those of us who are gathered here are fasting from one to seven days, depending on people's schedules and stamina. I will only be here for today and head back to Managua early tomorrow morning (to get ready to go back to the States). Sasamori has been drumming and praying since 6:00 and will continue this twelve hours a day for seven days....

Some base community people from Managua showed up during the afternoon in Dipilto to spend the night and walk the last day with us....In the evening as we gathered for our celebration, two more trucks showed up, one from Managua and the other from Waslala (a small town in the mountains northeast of Matagalpa, famous for its radical priest). The Waslala people had traveled for ten hours to join us at the border and changed their plans so they could stay through the all-night vigil on Saturday. They were carrying signs that said "For peace and democracy in the church!" in reference to their on-going conflict with Cardinal Obando....

The next morning...we set out to walk the last twelve kilometers to the border....The border is at the top of a ridge, so it was uphill all the way....When we arrived at the edge of the international zone, Chepita, who was up front as usual with the banner, knelt down in the road to pray silently for a few minutes. Of course this started the cameras clicking, but she ignored them and rose when she was ready. She has sixty-six years and many miles on her legs, yet managed to walk the entire distance from Managua to the border at Las Manos.

The celebration that followed was great. I was glad to see Pastora officiating. As usual we started with some singing and then moved into a couple minutes of silent reflection....The offering of symbols was very nice. First came Sasamori with his banner of the red sun and Japanese characters for his peace prayer....Chepita presented a Bible...Isabel presented her shoes, well worn, and talked about the need to keep struggling even when we are tired and worn out. Montserrat brought up a big paper peace crane. She talked about how we had been making them everywhere along the route, and how they were a symbol of our walk and our desire for peace....The last symbol to be presented was the cross of wood that had been decorated with palm branches, peace cranes and fresh flowers. George presented it and talked about how it was a symbol of resurrection and that it was also a symbol of death, that in the time of Jesus it was used to kill the insurrectionists. He then proceeded around the circle and asked everyone to lay their hands on it before he laid it at the border.

After this we had more singing, scripture reading and shared reflection. We ended with a kiss of peace (a part of Catholic mass). I wasn't able to hug everyone, but did make an effort to seek out Calixto, Raúl and others I had had bad feelings towards at different times on the walk....

One of the hardest parts of an experience like this is when it's over and the good-byes...have to be said. Some people left almost immediately after our arrival yesterday. Chepita, Francisco, Isabel and Raúl all left on a truck headed for Managua. Alicia left on the same truck to be dropped off in La Trinidad. As I hugged her she had tears streaming down her face.

Thursday, December 8, Mexico City

(The afternoon we arrived at the border) a Nicaraguan woman showed up to tell us about her daughter who had been kidnapped by the contras and to ask for our help. The incident had occurred six months previously, so all we could really do was listen....The woman had been following every lead possible to locate her daughter...and the pain and suffering was etched into her face. The girl is only fifteen. Having a child kidnapped and not knowing their status has got to be much worse than when you know they are dead and can grieve for them....

Sunday, December 11, Escondido, California

(Following the all-day vigil at the border on December 1) we had another celebration and prayer service....As soon as we started singing, some of the Nicaraguan *compas* (soldiers) from the border post came over to join the circle and a guy from the Honduran post came over from the other side as well. He obviously knew the Nicas....We welcomed them, expanded the circle so they could stand with us, and went on with the service.

The songs led into readings from scripture, the gospel passage being on the temptations in the desert. A Delegate of the Word (lay religious leader) from Waslala offered his reflections on this, then opened it up for a dialogue....I remember (the) Brazilian priest (who) said that the biggest temptation for

81

the Nicaraguans was to give up the struggle, to give in to the lure of a better life elsewhere. We had seen a lot of Nicas crossing the border during the day headed north....

More music followed this, with people singing in their respective languages (Spanish, English, Portuguese, Italian, Japanese, Catalonian)....The final prayer was shared by Sasamori and a Guatemalan woman...(who) prayed for people on both sides of the conflict, for increased compassion on the part of all of us....

The next morning I woke at about 5:00 A.M....I packed my gear and went up to sit with Sasamori for a while. He is another person that I don't know if or when I will see again, so I wanted to take advantage of the opportunity to sit with him and share in his prayers for peace. It was quite cold and windy there on top of the ridge as we sat together looking north into Honduras. After twenty minutes I rose to go, Sasamori gave me a long hug, and we parted....

Back down at the school (where we were staying), I said good-bye to the others who were heading up to join the vigil and left for Ocotal in the truck with Greg and a few others who were going in to buy vegetables and lemons for breaking the fast....I said good-bye to them at the market and went to the dirt-lot bus station to catch a bus down to Estelí....

AFTERWORD

We've now been back in the United States for over six months. We had gotten no further than San Diego when I received an offer to teach English at the community college in Bellingham, Washington, where a friend of mine had been an instructor. This was welcome news, as we were running low on money. Exactly a month after I finished teaching at the UCA, I was teaching a class of immigrants from all over the world who'd come to make a better life in the United States—including one young Nicaraguan woman who'd married an American businessman twice her age and was now in the process of bringing her entire family north. Our politics were different, but we nevertheless spent many happy moments reminiscing about toilet paper shortages, crowded buses, and the beauties of the Nicaraguan countryside.

For Peter and I found, contrary to what we'd thought when we were cursing the Managua heat, that coming back to the United States was *not* the same thing as coming home. We spent Christmas in the Seattle neighborhood where we'd lived for five years, attending Christmas Mass in our old parish there, which has always been a place of community and inspiration for us. But in those days, within two or three weeks of leaving Nicaragua, we could no longer see the things we had loved—all we could see was a shocking, excessive display of wealth. Even Mexico had seemed wealthy to us. As late as mid-March, I remember standing in a Bellingham supermarket looking at a heaping display of perfect, red-ripe tomatoes and bursting into tears because no one was paying attention to them.

In order to survive in Nicaragua, we'd had to change our

way of looking at the world. Now in order to survive in the United States, we had to change our eyes back. This process was slow, painful and made more difficult by the fact that we didn't want to lose the insight we'd gained in Nicaragua—nevertheless, it was unavoidable. By June of 1989, I was probably more similar to the person who'd left Seattle in January of 1988 than the one who'd left Managua in December. I have never liked big, shiny US supermarkets, but now they seem to me, once again, a normal part of existence. I take daily mail delivery, running water and working telephones for granted, and worry about saving money for a down payment on a house rather than about the price of tortillas this week. It's hard not to see the world through the eyes of those around you, and we have come to do so in the United States again as we had begun to in Nicaragua.

For since we've been back, we've had little contact with the people we left behind there—a few short letters, one or two phone calls. We've tried to send mail down with people who are travelling, but there are never very many of those, and to be any good to us, they have to be willing to deliver letters to obscure Nicaraguan addresses without street names or numbers ("from where the Hotel San Luis used to be, four blocks down and a half a block towards the lake"). We think of people there often, and talk about going back to Nicaragua to work some year (but not to Managua!)—however, unless we do, our contact will only grow more sporadic. If we return to Nicaragua in five years, how many of our friends will we be able to find? How much will they have changed? How much will we have changed? Will we have anything to say to each other?

In spite of our feelings of dislocation, of having changed worlds, there has been some continuity in our work. I'm still trying to look upon teaching as an opportunity for consciousness-raising between teachers and students, and have tried Freirian methods on my students here with mixed results. I have stayed in touch with my colleagues at the UCA who have continued working on our curriculum development project in the months since I left, and we're hoping to present our work at the big ESL convention in San Francisco next spring.

As for Peter, still inspired by the housing project we worked on in Puertas Viejas last July, he joined the local Habitat for Humanity group in Bellingham, and has been instrumental in helping them to complete their first home. It's definitely more difficult in the States to hang on to the vision of work being "for others," but that's one part of the revolutionary ideal that we hope never to lose.

I wish I could likewise say that we've thrown ourselves into Central American solidarity work since we've come back, but we haven't. Again, our activity in that regard has been sporadic and disorganized. Apparently our sense of anger at US policy towards Nicaragua and other countries in the region is not strong enough to contend with our lack of energy, our feelings of futility, and all the other reasons sensitive middle-class Americans have for not being politically involved. My hope is that as I once again begin to feel that I belong in this country, I will start taking more responsibility for its foreign policy. I owe Nicaragua that much, for having taught me so much.

Julia

JULIA WARWICK was born in California and grew up in rural British Columbia, where she went to a Quaker high school. Her parents, now Tibetan Buddhists, had been active in the anti-war movement of the 1960s. In 1979 she entered Evergreen State College in Olympia, Washington and became involved with the campaign against the Trident nuclear submarine base outside Seattle. This led to an involvement with two long-distance peace walks in 1980-81. On the second, which went from the Trident base to Washington, D.C., she met Peter Menard. They were married in 1982, and immediately joined the Jesuit Volunteer Corps and moved to Seattle. She was baptized a Catholic in 1983. From 1983-1987, Julia attended the University of Washington, receiving a BA in Japanese and a Masters in Teaching English as a Second Language. At the same time she learned Spanish and became involved with the movement to aid Central American refugees. In 1985, Julia and Peter travelled in Mexico and Central America and did human rights work in Guatemala.

PETER MENARD was born in Minnesota and grew up in suburban Connecticut, the third of twelve children in a Catholic family. He received an AA degree in Food Service Management in 1976, and then moved to the Boston area, where he discovered that he preferred carpentry to cooking. In 1979, he moved to the Sierra foothills of Northern California, where he spent one year building vacation homes and another year constructing a passive solar house for the local Catholic Worker Farm (the Catholic Worker is a radical movement started by Dorothy Day in the 1930s). In 1981 he walked across the country, and in 1982, after marrying Julia, he began working with Senior Services of Seattle in their Home Repair for the Elderly program. After one year as a Jesuit Volunteer there, he became a paid employee, remaining with the program through 1987.

COLOPHON

This book was set in Janson Text with
Futura Extra Bold display type by Carrie Greaves.

Design: Laurie Becharas